photographed and written by **Lou Jones**

interviews by **Lou Jones** and **Lorie Savel**

edited, with an introduction, by **Michael Radelet**

foreword by **Gerry Spence**

NORTHEASTERN UNIVERSITY PRESS

BOSTON

FINAL

EXPOSURE

PORTRAITS FROM DEATH ROW

Northeastern University Press

Copyright 1996 by Lou Jones

A Gallery Iso project.

Designed by
Christopher Passehl

Composed in Bauer Bodoni by Wellington Graphics, Boston, Massachusetts. Printed and bound by The Stinehour Press, Lunenberg, Vermont. The paper is Mead Moistrite Matte, an acid-free sheet.

Library of Congress
Cataloging-in-Publication Data

Jones, Lou, 1945–
  Final exposure : portraits from death row / photographs by Lou Jones ; interviews by Lou Jones and Lorie Savel ; edited, with an introduction, by Michael Radelet ; foreword by Gerry Spence.
    p. cm.
  ISBN 1-55553-277-2
  (pbk. : alk. paper)
  1. Death row inmates—United States—Case studies. 2. Death row inmates—United States—Pictorial works. I. Savel, Lorie. II. Radelet, Michael L. III. Title.
HV8699.U5J65   1996
364.6'6'092273—dc20
[B]   96-25544

MANUFACTURED IN THE
UNITED STATES OF AMERICA
00 99 98 97 96
5   4   3   2   1

To my father, for his opposition and love

To my mother, who discouraged me from adding

chocolate milk to my cereal, but encouraged everything else I pursued

Table of Contents

ix   Acknowledgments

xi   Foreword

xiii   Introduction

xvii   Authors' Prefaces

2   Harold Lamont "Wili" Otey

6   Edward Dean "Sonny" Kennedy

12   Mitchell L. Willoughby

16   Marko Bey

22   LaFonda Fay Foster

28   Walter Lee Caruthers

32   Philip Workman

36   Olen "Eddie" Hutchison

40   Gary Graham

45   James Lee Beathard

50   Robert West

56   Abdullah Bashir, a.k.a. Clifford Phillips

60   Lesley Lee Gosch

64   David Lee Powell

68   Jim Vanderbilt

72   Pamela Lynn Perillo

77   James H. Roane, Jr.

81   Jack Foster Outten, Jr.

85   Nelson Shelton

90   Nicholas Yarris

94   Mumia Abu-Jamal

99   Michael B. Ross

103   Terry Johnson

108   Daniel Webb

111   Duncan Peder McKenzie, Jr.

117   Lester Kills On Top

120   Vern Kills On Top

ACKNOWLEDGMENTS

In this project's infancy, three individuals extended invaluable support. We would like to thank Mike and Lisa Radelet and Wes Pomeroy for their unflagging belief in our vision.

The number of individuals and organizations who have championed this project has grown over time. The support of the following people has been essential to the success of this project. Paul Gagne, Jacqueline Humbert, Jamie DiVenere, Courtney Bent, Ian Tuck, Sarah Hunter, Ken MacEwen, Ali Miller, Kica Matos, Capital Case Network Attorneys, Lee Norton, Susan Cary, Sam Reese Sheppard, Vic Covalt, Bernard O'Donnell, Steven Hawkins, Enid Harlow, Ken Michaels, Al Politi, Howard Fisher, Skip Cohen, Tony Corbell, and Ron Gulaskey. The many organizations that lent their confidence and support include Amnesty International, the National Coalition to Abolish the Death Penalty, the NAACP Legal Defense and Educational Fund, Equal Justice, the State Case Resource Centers, the Eastman Kodak Company, Victor Hasselblad, Inc., and Polaroid.

Most important of all are the inmates who gave of themselves to participate in this project. All the individuals you will read about in this book made a remarkable leap of faith: they received a letter or a referral that requested that they allow three strangers to invade their space, photograph them, tape their words, and then tell their stories. They believed in our project and our intentions and entrusted us with their lives. We can never effectively thank them for their candidness and openness toward us.

We also wish to thank our editor at Northeastern University Press, Scott Brassart, to whom we are sincerely grateful for his continued confidence and belief in this project. The road to publication was long and bumpy, but Scott's support and patience were unending.

Finally, we want to thank Mike Radelet for his inspiring and poignant introduction. His input and insight are reflected throughout the pages that follow.

—Lou Jones and Lorie Savel

FOREWORD

I first saw the brave and beautiful photographs in this remarkable collection at my ranch near Dubois, Wyoming, one night when Lou Jones made a slide presentation to the young trial warriors at the Trial Lawyer's College. A silent pall fell over the small group. Few had ever looked in the face of a human being who was destined to be killed, purposely, with premeditation, on an hour and day certain. Now we looked at the faces, and what we saw from Jones's penetrating camera were not names or numbers, not writs of habeas corpus or titles on legal documents, but people: people who were living in abject terror, or who had no fear at all; who were resigned to their fate, or who felt sorrow and shame; who were confused and knew not what was happening to them, or who knew full well their fate and had long ago abandoned hope. We were shown people who had been touched by the camera, and who, in turn, touched us through the photographs.

I do not think a person can see the photographs in this book without a multitude of emotions being aroused. As I looked at the photographs I thought not only about Jones's artistry, but of its power: in the magical click of a shutter, he had captured the transient life that would so quickly be gone. I thought of the immortality a photo-graph can impart to a life, a life so seemingly worthless that it can be snuffed out nearly as quickly as the camera captures it forever. I thought about my own life, going quickly by, my own mortality, and how ungodly we play God with the lives of others. I thought about how an executioner goes from condemned to condemned with little more effort than my finger makes turning these pages. One man at a time, one page at a time, and their faces are gone. But neither the executioner nor the executed can ever go back. That is the horror of the death penalty, the horror that these photographs make palpable. Lou Jones cares, and his caring has been contagious: he has made me care and that is the final test of the photographer's eye.

—Gerry Spence

INTRODUCTION

In April 1991 I was on sabbatical leave from the University of Florida, working at the Family Research Laboratory at the University of New Hampshire. There I received a phone call from an old family friend, Wes Pomeroy. Wes is well known among criminal justice professionals; he once served as chief of police in Berkeley, California, and in 1969 he directed security for the Woodstock Music Festival. Wes had just returned from El Salvador, where, with a group of distinguished volunteers, he had helped to monitor that country's first democratic elections.

With Wes in El Salvador was photographer Lou Jones. During their week together, the two men found they had a common interest in criminal justice. Lou had recently been in Japan, and while there had seen a documentary describing the death penalty in the United States. The film had struck a chord in him, and he was thinking about how he might use his photography skills to shed some light on the issue. Wes knew that I had an interest in capital punishment, and he had encouraged Lou to contact me. Shortly after my talk with Wes, Lou and I met at his Boston studio.

Also at that meeting was Lorie Savel, who would soon become Lou's project manager; Ali Miller, then director of death penalty projects for Amnesty International U.S.A.; and my wife, Lisa, who had spent several years working with death-row inmates and attorneys in Texas before our marriage. That afternoon we spent several hours listening to Lou's ideas and helping to shape them, brainstorming new ideas, and learning more about one another's work. We all knew, though none of us mentioned it, that the probability of securing permission to work on death row was minuscule.

I soon learned that Lou Jones is one of the best commercial and art photographers in New England. Born and raised in Washington, D.C., Lou holds a B.S. in physics from Rensselaer Polytechnic Institute (1967) and has done graduate work in physics and computer science. But his life had changed in college when a roommate handed him a camera, and by 1971 he had decided to make photography his career. Today he and his staff of five work out of a studio in Boston's South End, where they specialize in location photography for corporate advertisements and collateral projects, like annual reports and calendars. Included on Lou's impressive list of clients are Nike, Federal Express, Mobil Oil, AT&T, Metropolitan Life, and Aetna Insurance. His assignments have taken him to almost every state in the United States and all over the world, earning him well over a million air miles. His photographs have been featured in *Time, Newsweek, National Geographic,* and *Esquire* and have won numerous professional awards.

Lorie Savel, who worked closely with Lou on this project, is a 1983 graduate of Smith College. She started working for Lou only six months before this project began. Told that her responsibilities would include the acquisition of commercial assignments and the packaging of exhibitions of Lou's work, she was surprised when her job expanded to include visits with condemned criminals. It's a long way from the offices of corporate decision makers to the bowels of death row. Today Lorie has probably been on more death rows than any other woman in the country.

We knew no photographs could be taken on death row without the consent of the inmates and their attorneys. Before approaching them, Lou worked to secure support for the project from some of the country's top defense attorneys and from key groups such as Amnesty International, the NAACP Legal Defense and Educational Fund, and the National Coalition to Abolish the Death Penalty. He and Lorie also formed an advisory committee of nationally renowned death-penalty activists and attorneys, who helped them to develop a detailed process for securing the inmates' informed consent. In the beginning, no one knew of a prison that would allow anyone to enter with

a camera. But the question for Lou and Lorie was never if their project could be done, but how. Eventually Lou confessed that he did not plan simply to take a small camera into prison; he needed permission to enter death row with enough photographic equipment to fill a mid-sized car.

From the start, however, the biggest challenge to entering death row was not the consent of the prisons, the inmates, or the attorneys, though those were formidable barriers. The biggest challenge was psychological: it is impossible to enter death row without thinking about the victims the inmates have left behind. Indeed, some take the position that to focus on death-row inmates is to demean the memory of their victims. But in a very real sense, this book is as much about victims as it is about offenders. One of the best ways to help the families of homicide victims, or the families of those killed by drunk drivers or any other senseless and avoidable means, is to take steps to reduce the occurrence of such tragedies in the future. Families of homicide victims want their communities to prevent others from going through the hell they have suffered. As I see it, only by understanding offenders—by recognizing their humanity, the fact that they are not that different from the rest of us—can we reduce the rates of criminal victimization.

The pages that follow will show that many death-row inmates have themselves been victimized—though certainly not in a way that negates their responsibility for their crimes. We know something about what causes people to become murderers. Many are victims of physical, sexual, or emotional abuse, of a lack of resources or responsible role models. Instead of talking about the justice of the death penalty, perhaps we ought to talk about the thousands of children who never get much of a chance in life. In this sense we all bear some responsibility for the high rates of violence that plague our society today.

The goal of this book is not to argue for the release from prison of condemned criminals. Some of the inmates described in this book are so pathological, our society could not have produced a more dangerous criminal had it tried. Rather, it is to suggest that even they should be understood as part of the human community. To understand crime, we must understand or at least acknowledge the humanity of criminals. There is an explanation for their criminality—a cause—and ignoring it will do nothing to prevent others from committing the same crimes. In his book *The Pursuit of Loneliness*, Philip Slater warned that in thinking about social problems, Americans should not assume that "unwanted difficulties, unwanted complexities and obstacles will disappear if they are removed from our immediate field of vision."[1]

So it is with our attitude toward convicted criminals. When the offender is dead, the problem is

gone. If evil resides inside the person, then getting rid of the person gets rid of the problem. But if that were true, we could rid society of criminal violence simply by killing all the criminals—or at least a few scapegoats. But the truth is, violent criminality is not a problem in itself, but a symptom of larger and more pervasive problems that threaten our social order. Executing the criminal removes only the symptom of these problems, and distracts our attention from the underlying causes. Though the death penalty is imposed in less than 3 percent of criminal homicides in the United States (and what separates those sentenced to death from others convicted of murder often has little to do with the heinousness of the offense), it allows us to pretend that we are actually doing something to reduce crime.

The pages of newspapers tell us the official version of crimes, and perhaps a little about the backgrounds of the perpetrators. Rarely do all parties to a crime agree on precisely what occurred, however, much less what caused the crime. What kind of person could have done this? we wonder. The question is never answered, and the reader is left to conclude that the accused is subhuman. It is easy to support the execution of those we consider subhuman; it is easy to kill someone who is simply a number.

But Lou's pictures show that even the worst criminals are human. Just as Amnesty International, whose symbol is a candle, spotlights human rights abuses, Lou's camera opens our eyes

[1] Philip Slater, *The Pusuit of Loneliness*

to the hidden reality of death row. He has only just scratched the surface. By the end of 1995 there were just over three thousand men and forty-nine women on death row in the United States. Hence, for every inmate whose story is told in this book, there are a hundred others whose stories we do not know.

Each photograph in this book is the end point of a long and unique journey. Before Lou could begin to shoot pictures, difficult questions had to be answered. How would administrators be convinced to open the prison gates and allow contact visits? How would prisoners be selected and approached? How could sympathetic photographs be taken without downplaying the magnitude of the offender's crime and dishonoring the memory of the victims? On average, each portrait in this book represents well over 150 hours of work.

Yet the process was not just one of overcoming bureaucracy or of fear of death row, but of becoming vulnerable to loss. Thinking about the death penalty is very different from looking into the eyes of a condemned person. Chatting with these people, getting to know them, forces you to come to grips with the reality of their crimes, and the punishment that awaits them. Accepting the official killing of a person you know is much more difficult than accepting the execution of a faceless villain, one you understand only in terms of his worst acts. As one inmate told Lorie, "You know, if the governor of this state or if anyone who thinks I should be dead would just spend one hour with me, they'd never be able to kill me." That is an overstatement, but there is much truth in it. Each picture in this book challenges us to see the human being in a criminal. It is not an easy challenge, but we must face it.

—Michael Radelet

AUTHORS' PREFACES

Every child is eventually weaned from his or her parents. The process can be delicate and natural, or it can be as painful and sudden as a jolt of electricity. At times it can be so gradual, so slow, that the growing distance between the parent and child cannot even be detected. Other times you can pinpoint the exact moment everything changes. That is how it is for me.

I was fourteen, maybe fifteen years old. My family was eating dinner and watching the television news. The anchorman reported that a convicted murderer had been executed early that morning. Daddy interrupted his meal to voice approval: "He got what he deserved." My father had made similar comments when the issue of capital punishment had arisen previously, and I had always agreed without question. But this time was different. This time I thought, "That's not right."

The day before, my father walked on water. He was indomitable, incorruptible, devoted, and an infinitely supportive man. Now he was wrong. I've never mentioned it to him, but thirty years later his words still flow like sweet poison in my blood. This schism is probably his finest gift to me. It is the first time that I, the son, disagreed with him, the father.

I have carried my moral opposition to capital punishment with me throughout my life, and it is this opposition that led me into undertaking such an unusual project.

—Lou Jones

When Lou first approached me six years ago with the idea of photographing death-row inmates, I though he was crazy. I don't think either of us realized what we were in for. All we really knew was that he wanted unrestrained access to death-row prisoners, and that it was my job to get it. Neither of us knew anyone in prison, let alone on death row. Nor were we acquainted with any criminal justice lawyers, corrections officials, investigators, or activists. Six years later, it seems as if we know no one else.

Gaining access to death row is not easy under any circumstances, and nearly impossible if such access means an in-the-flesh visit by three people toting a tape recorder and nine trunks of photographic equipment. The situation becomes further complicated when one of the three visitors is a woman. Even worse, it was essential for our purposes that we meet the inmates face to face, without barriers or restraints of any kind.

Each state, each institution, each inmate, and each lawyer had a different agenda, different rules. Each had to be carefully maneuvered. In some states our contact with death-row inmates was the first ever granted. Even when this wasn't the case, access had previously been limited to shackled inmates held behind wire mesh or thick, bulletproof glass. Many of the men and women we photographed hadn't been allowed to touch their own children since becoming incarcerated. For a few that meant eighteen or even twenty years.

We began with the task of identifying potential subjects, but worried they might not respond to our letters. Death-row inmates get interview requests from the media all the time. How could we get them to acknowledge our requests? How could we get them to trust us? Lou and I also felt we needed to be careful when crafting our letters so as to communicate our intentions to the inmates without arousing suspicions of prison officials, who could be reading the letters first.

The initial contact, a task that seemed so difficult, proved to be only the start of a lengthy, sometimes painful process. Convincing prisons to break long-standing rules on behalf of a lone photographer with no press affiliation was even more difficult than we'd earlier imagined.

To illustrate this point I will provide two examples. First, Texas. We were referred to several inmates on Texas's death row by Lisa Radelet. Lisa spent years working at Ellis I in Huntsville and provided many helpful leads. We wrote to six men Lisa suggested and heard back from all of them within a few months. One response led to a seventh inmate. We were ecstatic, but conservatively so, as we could go to Ellis I only on "media day." On media day reporters are allowed to interview inmates in a small room, with barriers between inmates and interviewers. Everyone meets at the same time. There are no exceptions.

This would not do for us. We needed a contact visit—no barriers—and we needed to see the inmates one at a time. We had only one card to play. Lou knew a U.S. congressman who we thought might be willing to intervene on our behalf. In the midst of negotiating with the congressman, we received word that Gary Graham, a Texas inmate, was scheduled to be executed the next week. We not only needed assistance, we needed immediate assistance. Lou's congressman friend complied by faxing a letter to the Texas Department of Corrections expressing enthusiasm for the project. Our feet were in the door.

The director of the Department of Corrections called me after receiving the fax, telling me I was crazy, there was no way we could get onto Ellis I, and certainly no way we could get in the way we hoped. I somehow changed his mind; after an endless phone conversation he agreed to allow us into the prison to photograph Gary Graham that Friday, just a few days before his scheduled execution. Unfortunately for the project but fortunately for the studio, Lou had a commercial assignment already scheduled for that day. I asked the director for access at seven o'clock in the evening, well past visiting hours and not the best time for disruptions; prison staff is limited in the evening. Lou and I couldn't believe he agreed.

Yet there was work still to do. We needed the director to allow us to photograph Graham without shackles, and to agree to let us back inside at a later date to photograph the remaining six inmates, also without shackles. I telephoned the director night and day, and we were soon on a first-name basis. Finally, he consented. We photographed Gary Graham that Friday, without restraints, and without incident. The director granted us a two-day visitation two weeks later to meet with the six other inmates, and gave us the run of the prison infirmary to conduct our business.

Pennsylvania presented a different set of battles. We had heard from Pamela Tucker, a case resource worker, that one of the state's death-row inmates planned to get married. Pamela thought including the marriage as part of our project might be a good idea. The prison disagreed. Officials expressed little willingness to disrupt the operation of their facility and told us to give up, that there was no way we would ever get in.

We missed the wedding, but continued to correspond with the inmate, Nicholas Yarris, after his marriage. We received many letters and many collect phone calls. We felt as if we were getting to know Nicholas and that he had begun to trust us. Yet we also felt powerless because no matter what we tried, we couldn't get in to photograph him. We placed Pennsylvania on hold until, more than a year later, we received a letter from Steve Hawkins, then at the NAACP Legal Defense Fund. They had heard about our project and felt one of their clients, Mumia Abu-Jamal, should be included.

We re-approached the Pennsylvania Department of Corrections, this time with the weight of the NAACP behind us. But even with the NAACP's clout and connections, we still came up short. It seemed as if we'd never get onto Pennsylvania's death row. Then, six months later, the chain of command at the prison changed. We decided to make one more effort. This time the prison relented. We were in. But officials informed us that in the entire history of the prison no one had been allowed to visit unshackled inmates without a glass or wire-mesh barrier. State policy. We would not be an exception.

I called the director in Texas, hoping he would vouch for us and tell Pennsylvania that we'd photographed and interviewed seven of Texas's inmates, unshackled and without barriers, without incident. He agreed and called his Pennsylvania counterpart. We were dumbfounded. Two years of work came together in a single telephone call. Not only could we photograph Nicholas Yarris and Mumia Abu-Jamal, but we would use the prison's conference room. Our persistence paid off again.

When this project began the paperwork occupied a single file. Now it fills an entire file cabinet. Our best estimate is that gaining access to each of the twenty-seven individuals we photographed took about 150 hours: 150 hours of rejection and frustration multiplied by twenty-seven individuals equals 4050 hours just to get in. Would we do this again? I'd like to think so. This experience has had a significant impact on my life. I used to think these people should all die. Now I see that compassion and humanity have no barriers. Now we need to invest in our children, to prevent their ever getting this far. Many of these men and women came to be where they are not because of one experience but because of the circumstances of their entire lives.

If you read this book and if you examine the photographs, I hope you will see human beings. If their humanity presents a dilemma for you, then the act of killing any one will seem incomprehensible.

—Lorie Savel

FINAL

EXPOSURE

Harold Lamont "Wili" Otey

Nº 31840

Nebraska State Penitentiary   Lincoln, Nebraska

Year of birth   1952
Marital status   single
Children   none
Date of offense   June 11, 1977
Sentenced to death   June 20, 1978
Status   executed September 3,
                         1994, by electrocution

Harold Lamont Otey was convicted of the rape and murder of twenty-six-year-old Jane Mc-Manus in her Omaha apartment. According to the state, Otey entered the apartment in the middle of the night and removed a stereo. When he reentered to remove other items, McManus awoke. Otey raped McManus, then stabbed and finally strangled her with a belt.

Arrested six months later in Florida, Otey confessed to the crime but later recanted. At trial he was represented by an inexperienced attorney just two years out of law school; the state was represented by the most experienced homicide prosecutor in Nebraska. Otey spent seventeen years on death row. In 1994 his appeal for clemency was denied, and he was executed.

Source: *State v Otey*, 187 NW2d 36 (1979); Larry Myers, "An Appeal for Clemency," in *The Death Penalty in America*, 4th ed., ed. Hugo Adam Bedau (1996).

I knew exactly where I was going: 40 degrees 49 minutes north latitude, 96 degrees 41 minutes west longitude. After a night of bad dreams in a sleazy motel, I drove up the interstate toward Lincoln and the Nebraska State Penitentiary. In my anxiety, I got there thirty minutes early. Wili Otey was the first death-row inmate I would be allowed to photograph, so I had no idea what to expect. I don't mind admitting I was scared. I held my breath the whole time.

I can remember even now every sight and smell along the way. After walking through a metal detector and passing a security search, I was shown into an empty room with a blackboard. The guard gave no hint as to protocol or what I should expect. Then Wili strode through the door, with a stack of textbooks under his arm . . . *alone* I was in the same room with a convicted murderer. This was no longer theoretical. I panicked; I didn't know what to say. But Wili's quiet confidence helped me to regain my equilibrium. As I listened, he told stories—of betrayal by the press, of friends who had championed his cause. Slowly, I realized he was not the person I thought he was. I would never again fall into that trap with my subjects.

Illiterate when he was convicted, Wili, or "Walkin' Willie" (a nickname he got as a handler on the horse-racing circuit) was now articulate and well read. (His college education had been paid for by the state.) Wili had mastered the English language well enough to write poetry, and had published three books of his verse. He was now a model prisoner with unique privileges: the guards were so comfortable with him, he could move about the prison unescorted. Like many other prisoners, after years in jail Wili had undergone such a dramatic transformation, he was no longer the same person who had committed the crime he was being punished for. Even the prison administrators admitted Wili was a changed person.

The state was having a hard time getting rid of Wili. He had proven to be a worthy adversary. His story had remained on the front page for years because of media blitzes from the local press and TV newsmagazines. Pressure had been mounting to reinstate executions in Nebraska—the last had been in 1963—and the state's largest newspaper, the *Omaha World-Herald*, had been relentless in demanding his death. While most death-row inmates desire to slip into the safety of obscurity, Wili had chosen to fight back, with help from friends and supporters all over the U.S.

Wili eventually lost his battle. In return for clemency, the governor of Nebraska demanded that Wili show remorse for an act he claimed he didn't do. Wili refused. On September 3, 1994, at one minute past midnight, Harold "Wili" Otey made history. He became the first man to be electrocuted in the state of Nebraska in thirty-one years. He maintained his innocence to the end.

an impractical reality (death poem)

could you walk unescorted to your
    death
could you pass that group of
    strangers and not bat an eye
could you ingest the volt and volts
    that make you jerk and contort and
    not cry out
could you wait years and years
    envisioning you strapped in that
    chair
would you ever close your eyes afraid
    you missed a moment of life
would you give a damn that they
    murdered you
would you care
i say i will not flinch
will not sob
will not faint
i say i will not ask anyone i love(d) to
    be there
will not eat their offering of a special
    meal
will not write anybody good-bye
i say i will not want any tears shed
will not hear any prayers
will not beg any god to save me
i say drink wine and dance/party
when they murder me
'cause the next time
i say
it will be you.

—Wili Otey

from his book *Sing for Mooncrumbs*

EDWARD DEAN "SONNY" KENNEDY

Nº 066680

Florida State Prison   Starke, Florida

Year of birth	1945
Marital status	single
Children	none
Date of offense	April 11, 1981
Sentenced to death	January 12, 1982
Status	executed July 21, 1992, by electrocution

Edward Dean Kennedy was sentenced to life imprisonment in 1978, for the murder of a motel clerk in Miami. He was confined at Union Correctional Institution in Raiford, barely a quarter of a mile from Florida State Prison in Starke, where the state's electric chair is housed. On April 11, 1981, Kennedy escaped with two companions, but his friends were quickly recaptured. To steal a change of clothes, Kennedy broke into a trailer home a few dozen miles from the prison. While he was there, the owner, Floyd H. Cone, Jr., returned home with his cousin, Florida Highway Patrol Trooper Robert C. McDermon. Ironically, Cone and McDermon had gone to the trailer to pick up weapons in order to join the search for Kennedy. When McDermon saw Kennedy, he fired his weapon; Kennedy returned the fire with a shotgun and a rifle he had found in the trailer. Both McDermon and Cone were killed in the gunfight. Kennedy then fled to a neighboring trailer, taking a woman and her six-month-old baby as hostages for about an hour before he surrendered.

Source: Kennedy v State, 455 So2d 351 (1984); New York Times, 22 July 1992; United Press International, 4 December 1981, 14 April 1981, 12 April 1981.

My first meeting with Ed "Sonny" Kennedy was through the U.S. Mail, a twenty-nine-cent rendezvous. In the spring of 1992 we met and soon became pen pals. Reams of blue-lined yellow legal paper unfolded his story to me. At the time, Ed's death warrant was imminent; though I didn't know it, he had only a few weeks to live. I got to know him very fast.

The similarities in our lives bonded us. He was born just a few blocks from my Boston studio. We were the same age; we even looked alike. At times I couldn't tell where his personality left off and mine began. We shared an interest in art, music, and politics. It seemed as if our lives had begun together, diverged, then converged again in Florida State Prison. I had gone to college; he had gone to hell. Though our correspondence lasted only a few months, we became close friends. The absence of time, I suppose, can compress as easily as the passage of time, producing diamonds.

Ed was sentenced to death for killing a police officer and a civilian during his escape from a correctional institution where he was serving a life sentence for an earlier killing. In the first incident,

Ed had been surprised when his partner shot the victim. After the second, Ed claimed self-defense:

The newspapers will tell you that I gunned these people down, but it wasn't like that. It was a gun battle.

An escaped murderer, Ed quickly realized that he was wanted dead or alive. The men were looking for him, and he panicked. The death penalty is inevitable for a prison escapee and three-time killer, especially in Florida.

While on death row Ed had written to several colleges, offering to tell his life story, but none had ever responded. He worried that his mistakes might be his only legacy, and wanted to help others avoid the errors he had made. Perhaps he agreed to be photographed because he felt it might help someone—anyone. He entrusted with me the responsibility of seeing that his story would not be forgotten.

When he was younger, Ed had been an accomplished saxophonist. He had taught himself to play the instrument between his many prison sentences. In our letters we often talked about our shared love of music, especially jazz. He liked Coltrane; I liked Miles Davis. Though prison had denied him both the instrument he needed to play and the equipment he needed to listen, he retained the ability and desire to talk about it.

It took me into another world . . . a world of freedom and beauty. I was free. This was back in the seventies and music at that time was like a refuge. It was a place where I could cast off all the pain and misery and get free from the oppression and all of the other shit . . . the racism and all that. So, it was a refuge . . . a place where I could go and find peace. And when I played, I got into my own world. It was a world of freedom and beauty. I could go in the park and practice all day.

When I went to photograph Ed, our few hours together flew by. The prison had agreed to my visit on the condition that our time together be limited. For some reason, the guards allowed us to exceed the specified time, perhaps knowing how little time Ed had left.

A few weeks later Ed asked me to return for his electrocution. Going back there was one of the hardest decisions I've ever made. I counted on inept air traffic control to spare me from the ordeal of being present when Ed died. But on this trip, everything fell into place. I left death row in Kentucky, where I had just completed another shoot, and arrived in a holding cell in Florida just hours before the execution. The doors to the prison had been sealed, but I pleaded to be let in.

I remember few things from that visit besides setting up the tape recorder. This mental lapse drives me crazy, though I know it's all on tape. Everything happened in slow motion. We talked around frivolous topics but soon the excess gravity pulled us back to reality.

They don't care about people like me. People like me, black people, minorities, poor whites, they don't mean anything to people like that. . . . We are just a nuisance.

In that room, in my mind, Ed Kennedy defined himself. Then the guards unlocked his handcuffs, and in desperation I broke a prison rule—no physical contact—and threw my arms around Ed. "It will be all right," he said, sensing my discomfort. You cannot say good-bye on death row.

The guards pulled us apart. They grabbed his hands and pinned them behind his back. Then they led him to the death chamber.

As the time for the execution drew nearer, the scene outside the prison became more frenetic. On one side of the yellow-tape barrier, protesters held candles and swayed to a silent chant. On the other, partiers in ten-gallon hats pulled Budweisers from a cooler. When the hearse drove away from the prison, a cheer went up from the crowd. And then, right above the room where Ed had died, a rainbow appeared.

A few months later, much too early on a Monday morning, the telephone rang and an old friend revealed to me that he had done time with "Sonny" in the state prison at Walpole, Massachusetts. He had seen some of my photographs in a newspaper article. "Ed was a bank robber," he told me. "The best. He learned while we were in Walpole." He described how they would lie on the tailor-shop cutting tables contemplating the perfect crime. "He had millions stashed away."

Ed Kennedy died at the age of forty-eight. Until that moment I had been naive enough to hope that my photographs would throw a kind of safety net over the few condemned individuals I had photographed. He was the first person I knew to be executed, but he would not be the last.

I'm downstairs right next door to the death chamber where the electric chair is. Tomorrow morning they'll take me out there, strap me to the chair and kill me . . . tomorrow morning at seven o'clock. I'm in the cell right next . . . right in the back of the death chamber.

MITCHELL L. WILLOUGHBY

Nº 82148 6-G-4

Kentucky State Penitentiary   Eddyville, Kentucky

Year of birth   1959

Marital status   divorced prior to conviction

Children   three

Date of offense   January 13, 1983

Sentenced to death   August 30, 1983

Status   under appeal

Mitchell L. Willoughby was convicted with Leif Halvorsen of three counts of murder, two of which brought death sentences. A codefendant, Susan Hutchens, received a ten-year term in exchange for testifying against the two men. The victims had been shot during a drug-related argument at a home in Lexington, Kentucky. Two bodies were found on a bridge, each bound to a heavy rock. A third was found in the river below the bridge.

Source: *Willoughby v Commonwealth*, 730 SW2d 931 (1987); United Press International, 18 December 1986, 23 January 1986, 31 August 1983; Associated Press, 15 January 1983.

Early one morning in 1992, a corrugated box arrived in the mail at my Boston studio. I did not immediately recognize the Kentucky postmark, or the name on the return address. The package turned out to be a macabre calling card. Mitchell Willoughby, a prisoner we had written to, had sent one of his handmade sculptures. Well crafted, it was a miniature figure sitting in the electric chair, faithful to the smallest detail. I was not amused. But rejecting him for his perverse sense of humor would be missing the point. So, I wrote back.

The gift turned out to be a test. How Mitchell Willoughby would react to my request to photograph him depended on how I would respond to his gift. From inside his prison, Mitchell was trying to screen out the tourists. My letters struck the right chord. With a minimum of preparation I was off to Eddyville, where the new Kentucky State Penitentiary stood.

The Kentucky State Penitentiary was one of the few prisons where I was allowed on death row. The state is very proud of its brand-new facility. Once inside, I was introduced to everyone. Some of the inmates were dressed in shorts and T-shirts; others, stepping out of the shower, were wrapped only in towels. Slowly, one by one, the guards and administrators were called away. In the commotion the metal door was closed, and I found myself with Ian Tuck, my assistant, outnumbered by the prisoners.

The inmates usually busied themselves with pool, checkers, chess, and a Universal workout machine, but today we were the live entertainment. In the cavernous common room, dozens of men milled around, wandering in and out of their cells. Everyone moved in slow motion. There was movement in all the dark places. Even the shadows had eyes. Mitchell talked, and though no one seemed to listen, I am quite sure everyone heard. To rid myself of the eerie feeling of being watched,

take their recreation. There again, small groups of men pretended not to be interested in the celebrity inflicted on one of their own, but their eyes followed every move we made.

Mitchell Willoughby is a big man. He lifts weights and practices Tae Kwon Do when no one is looking (the martial arts are illegal in prison). Soft spoken, he didn't talk much; when he did, his comments were usually monosyllabic.

Mitchell admits to killing three people. He and a friend went to collect some money that was owed them in a drug deal. Things didn't go as planned; they didn't just get their money and move on. Instead, they quarreled with the debtor and ended up killing him and two of his friends. In a panic, they drove the bodies to a nearby bridge and tried to dump them in the river. The combination of drugs and anger was deadly.

I concentrated on the work at hand. Making a subject comfortable in front of a camera is a daunting task. It takes a while for the person to get used to me and begin to ignore my presence. With everyone in the cellblock looking on, we struggled to put Mitchell and ourselves at ease.

I was excited to be able to include some of Mitchell's surroundings and fellow prisoners in my photographs. We did not often get that chance. Later we were even allowed to take Mitchell outside to the "yard," where prisoners

Mitchell's partner in crime shares the same cellblock; we talked with him briefly about his family. While we were speaking, we were interrupted by a man who we later found out had been on death row longer than anyone else in the United States. He had been sentenced to die in 1960, but the death penalty had been declared unconstitutional. Afraid of living among the general prison population, he had refused to leave death row. The state of Kentucky didn't know what to do with him. Shortly after we met, he died of natural causes. No one has been executed in Kentucky since 1962.

MARKO BEY

CN861-78241

New Jersey State Penitentiary   Trenton, New Jersey

Year of birth	1965
Marital status	single
Children	none
Date of offense	April 26, 1983
Sentenced to death	December 15, 1983
Status	under appeal

In December 1983 Marko Bey was sentenced to death for the rape and murder of nineteen-year-old Cheryl Alston. Her nude and battered body was found in a vacant lot near the boardwalk in Ocean City, New Jersey. In 1984 Bey received a second death sentence for sexually assaulting and strangling forty-six-year-old Carol Peniston. Bey was seventeen at the time of the first murder; he turned eighteen just two weeks before the second. In addition to his confession, abundant physical evidence tied him to both crimes.

Source: *State v Bey*, 645 A2d 685 (1994), 610 A2d 814 (1992), 548 A2d 887 (1988), 548 A2d 846 (1988); *New York Times*, 29 September 1984, 16 December 1983.

In November 1990 I read an article in *Vanity Fair*, about four men who had been convicted of serial murder in California. The story described their daily routines and interaction. But the photographs that accompanied it confused the portrait the author had drawn. Small and grainy, they made the perpetrators look crazed and insidious. The implication was deceptive. Those pictures gave me the incentive to photograph death row.

In June 1992 I wrote a letter to Marko Bey, one of three men residing on death row in New Jersey.

I just got off the phone with Jim Stone [Bey's lawyer] to learn that you are interested in having me come down to Trenton to meet and possibly photograph you. I thought it might be a good idea to write and explain what it is that we are involved in.

I am a photographer based out of Boston. I thought you might be interested in seeing some of my work and I have therefore enclosed some printed promotional materials so that you can see the quality and care I take in it. I am also enclosing a photograph of one of the participants in this project [Wili Otey] so that you can get a feeling for what I am trying to accomplish with these images.

Basically, the idea is to give you an identity, and to tell your story through a sensitive photographic portrayal. The "magic" of photography still amazes me after all these years. I have seen people form immediate bonds with pictures and I am trying to make my photographs communicate so that happens more and more often. If I am successful an entire story can be told without words.

In July Bey acknowledged receipt of my letter.

I'm against the D.P. but because of other reasons not only the obvious. No one has the right to knowingly take a persons life. (To plan to end life is wrong no matter what the reason) I also disagree with Anti-Abortionists. In one sense they say they are against: The taking of life (unborn child) but life is life unborn or born so why do Anti-Abortionists support the D.P. I am myself against Abortion BUT I or any man who can not get pregnant nor a woman who isn't pregnant has the right to vote on or tell a woman who is pregnant what to do with her body. And I am speaking from experience. Also Environmentalist is into protecting all wild life but don't help protect Human Life. . . .

Anyway Death Row is a lonely place. . . .

Two weeks later I wrote back to tell him we were in the process of gaining permission to see him.

Your willingness however to communicate with me and to discuss whatever topic or topics you feel may be helpful to the development of this project are very important. This is important in terms of me getting to know you; to learn

about what's important to you, what matters. What you care about . . .

On August 28 Lorie Savel, project manager for my studio, entered death row for the first time. Her role was to interview Marko Bey on tape. Outside the visiting room she panicked, unsure what she should say. My advice was to treat Marko like anyone else; he probably hadn't been treated like a human being for a long time.

A last-minute snafu set up a debate over the appropriateness of removing the handcuffs from the prisoner. We had to sign a waiver absolving the state of New Jersey of liability. Finally Marko Bey, one of only three people on death row in New Jersey at the time, entered the room. He was suspicious, his speech terse and barely audible, with a slight stutter.

When I was young, my aunt gave me a black kitten. He grew into a big, lumbering alley cat and ruled the neighborhood. Wily and street-smart, he came home whenever he pleased. If you rubbed him the wrong way he would bite you, just enough to exhibit his displeasure. Marko Bey reminded me of that cat, dark and brooding.

I busied myself setting up lights, loading cameras, changing perspective. Lorie persisted in trying to draw Bey out. She was careful not to talk about his case. (This was our first audio recording, and we feared it might be subject to subpoena.) I listened to the conversation, chiming in every once in a while to make my presence known.

Later, when I reviewed the tapes, I realized we had learned very little. Marko had rambled on and on, never really finishing a thought.

During our meeting with Bey, we learned that Rob Marshall, the subject of the best selling book *Blind Faith*, was doing time with him. Marshall's case was infamous. According to the newspapers, he and his wife had gone to the theater. After the show, Marshall had pulled their car into a poorly lit rest area, saying he needed to check for a flat tire, and supposedly murdered her. He was seriously in debt at the time, and his wife's life was insured. I heard from him in August 1992.

I received your name from Marko Bey. He told me you wrote to me; unfortunately, I did not receive your letter. I believe I would be interested in your program; please send me the pertinent information at your convenience.

Thank you.

In November 1992 I received another letter from Marshall.

Please accept my apologies for not replying sooner. I have been trying to convince my lawyers to approve a photo session but have been unsuccessful. They apparently understand your concept but do not think it would be in my best interest to become involved at this time. If their position changes, I will be in touch.

Thank you for your interest.

The next month I wrote to Marko Bey.

Today, Lorie and I finally had the opportunity to select images from your shoot to print and as soon as we get them back we will get them off to you right away. Hopefully, in time for Christmas.

On Sunday we leave for Tennessee. We've been given approval to go in and photograph three men on death row. We couldn't get approval to photograph them all together but we are allowed to visit and photograph all three of them in one day.

A few weeks ago we received a letter from an inmate in Missouri and he included a newsletter, which is published in England, called *Lifelines*. The newsletter is distributed among death-row inmates in the U.S. (kind of odd that a resource for U.S. death-row inmates has to develop outside of the U.S.). Enclosed is a copy of the newsletter, which you may want to subscribe to. You'll notice a section of this newsletter asking inmates if they are interested in pen pals. Hope this is useful.

Six months later Bey wrote to me that politics was increasing the population on death row.

This wing now has 7 occupant's as of this letter. Unfortunately, this is a election year for Governor in January, so it's likely that more will be sent to this wing.

In April 1994 Bey wrote me a chatty letter about the book *Dead Man Walking*, by Sister Helen Prejean. He gave the address of the prison chaplain, and speculated about his most recent appeal.

My second appeal was heard 8 months ago, so I'm looking for a ruling on that appeal any day now. The main force of this appeal is on racism playing a part in my case. . . . The court at the D.A.'s seemed to be worried that racism was a factor (cause) of the jury giving me the D.P. . . .

The next month Lorie returned his letter.

The book you mentioned by Sister Helen Prejean *(Dead Man Walking)* is great. We've both read it and commend her ability to deal with the issues and emotions surrounding the death penalty and the human beings involved. She effectively deals with the issues in a way that would be nonthreatening to pro–death-penalty believers. Which is really the point, isn't it? The primary goal should be to change the minds of those who are pro, not to further confirm the beliefs of the anti–death-penalty believers. Certainly, it's great to accomplish both if you can find a way to get the pro thinkers to open their minds to what you're trying to communicate. If it's nonthreatening they'll see the facts, the issues and the emotions more clearly and openly and hopefully consider their position.

Last year we had the opportunity of meeting her. She spoke at an awards meeting of the Massachusetts Citizens Against the Death Penalty. She spoke of her book and her ability to change the minds of many who have read the book: our goal with this project as you know. She's a great inspiration to the potential successes.

In April we gave a lecture at the Photographic Resource Center here in Boston about the project. It's one of the most well-known photo resources in the state. Over 200 people came to the lecture, and we have received a lot of feedback. One designer who went to the lecture said she came to it knowing exactly how she felt. She was pro–death-penalty. She left the lecture not only against the death penalty but against the criminal justice system. . . .

By August 1995, our relationship with this at-first suspicious prisoner was close enough for Lorie to write the following announcement:

Anyway, my great news is that on February 9, 1995, I gave birth to a six-pound, nine-ounce baby boy. We named him Chason Scott. His nickname is Chase. I never could have imagined how wonderful being a mom is. It's just incredible and he is terrific.

LaFonda Fay Foster

Fayette County Detention Center
Lexington, Kentucky

Year of birth	1963
Marital status	divorced prior to crime
Children	none
Date of offense	April 23, 1986
Sentenced to death	April 24, 1987
Status	pending sentence

LaFonda Fay Foster and a codefendant, Tina Hickey Powell, were convicted of killing five acquaintances after a four-day binge of drinking and intravenous cocaine injections. Trouble began when the women ran short of money to buy more drugs. They went to a friend's house and persuaded her and her husband, the housekeeper, and two of the husband's friends to go out with them to cash a check. After a couple of hours of driving around Lexington, Powell and Foster ordered the five passengers out of the car and forced them to lie face down in the grass. They shot two of the victims there—one of whom died after being stabbed and dragged "for a considerable distance" under the car.

After stopping at a bar and getting more bullets, Foster and Powell drove to a loading dock behind a paint store, where they stabbed and shot a second victim and ran over the body with the car. A few hours later they took the three remaining victims to a deserted field, shot them in their heads, stabbed them repeatedly, cut their throats, and ran over them with the car. They then set the car ablaze. The two women were arrested shortly thereafter at a nearby hospital, where they had gone to clean up and hail a cab.

At trial the women admitted their guilt. Because Powell claimed Foster had coerced her into committing the murders, the jury recommended she be sentenced to life imprisonment. The judge accepted the recommendation. Despite evidence of an extremely abusive childhood, and the fact that the killings were drug-induced, Foster was sentenced to death. But because the trial judge refused to hold separate hearings before sentencing the defendants, in 1991 the Kentucky Supreme Court vacated Foster's death sentence. At the end of 1995, a hearing for a new sentence had not yet been held.

Source: *Foster v Commonwealth*, 827 SW2d 670 (1991); United Press International, 27 April 1987, 24 April 1987, 20 March 1987.

There are few women on death row in the United States today, perhaps because jurors can sympathize with women, find it difficult to see them as dangerous, and give them the benefit of the doubt. Those women who do inhabit the Row tend to be more isolated than their male counterparts. Most refuse to talk with outsiders. Yet from the beginning, we felt a special need to include women among those we photographed. Thus we were elated when Kevin McNally, one of the country's top death-penalty defense attorneys and Fay Foster's pro bono lawyer, gave us permission to meet his client.

What would a young woman on death row be like? Demure? Overpowering? Scary? Scared? We knew that Fay, one of the most notorious murderers in Kentucky, had gone on her drug-induced crime spree only a few days after finishing a jail term for minor offenses. Although Fay's life had never been exemplary, she had no history of violent behavior. The physical and sexual abuse she endured as a child undoubtedly contributed to her drug abuse and outlaw lifestyle. Fay Foster is a woman hardened by the hateful experiences of youth.

My world kind of revolved around my father and I thought that if I loved him enough that maybe he would change and he would love me, too. . . . He's very cold hearted. He doesn't care about me and I finally accepted that. . . . I'm not as defensive when it comes to him now, and I accept that he is like he is but I choose not to let him be a part of my life emotionally or whatever.

Some say Fay was trying to kill her father the night she went on her rampage. She has little memory of it.

To take us to Fay, the guards led us back into the bowels of the prison to the cramped little cubicle that is her cell. We brushed past female prisoners who didn't know why we were there, trying to ignore their stares. We weren't welcome there; they wanted us to know it. Once past their scrutiny, we entered Fay's home, "a mattress inside a toilet."

Fay looked very fragile when we entered the room—so close to the edge, I didn't think she would finish the interview. She had demanded that her lawyer be present; he acted as a buffer between us. Fay Foster trusted Kevin McNally as she had no other man. Men had given her little reason to trust them before now. The session began uncomfortably. Fay glanced furtively toward Kevin for approval or reassurance. There was a slight vibrato to her voice. After several shrugs of Kevin's shoulders, Fay began to talk about her addiction.

I think the worst thing about me being a junkie was that I lost my spirit, for life and people. Because I like people, in general, I do. . . .

Nevertheless, the opportunity to tell her own story was important to Fay. Like many other prisoners we interviewed, she complained that the media had no interest in her point of view. Since her arrest the press had portrayed her as a hardened degenerate.

Before her crime, Fay had existed on guile, and was now silent about the things she did to survive on the streets. Suffice it to say, they ran the gamut. Fay often suffered just because of the company she kept.

And the next thing you know you're hiding your face because one of your friends has ripped everybody off in one bar and they think you're like that, too. Or she done sucked somebody's wong-wong under the table.

After we met, Fay sent me videotapes of her arrest and trial. They are like scenes from a made-for-TV movie. But Fay's life in prison is just as hard as her life on the streets was.

Violence . . . is a token given in exchange for respect and that's how it is on the streets, too. You know, you give people their "props." In other words, you congratulate them for making some kind of criminal move. That's how it is in the ghettos. . . . I don't know how else to say it.

This is not bravado; Fay is every bit as hard as her words. She has to be to survive in prison. A short time after our visit, one of Fay's friends cut herself in a fit of jealousy and let some of her blood drip into Fay's coffee cup. The woman is HIV positive. Fay had to be transferred because of the feud.

Sharing her feelings was new to Fay. It was not a comfortable experience for her.

I feel a lot more now than I used to. . . . I don't have as many defenses as I used to, OK? And when I start to really feel my pain and my remorse and having to spend the rest of my life in the penitentiary, then I get overwhelmed by those emotions and I still haven't learned to work through them without crashing . . . just living in despair a week or two after that.

Personal appearance is very important to Fay; in her life outside prison, her existence had depended on it. She complained to us about the ugly uniforms prisoners wore, the compromises she was forced to make. She has found clever ways of coping.

I wear brown vitamins. I use that for my eyeliner and Kool Aid for my blush. Or, the red-orange vitamins, I use that for my blush since the Kool Aid started breaking my face out. And since I take vitamins every day, I eat whatever I use.

Fay somehow manages to live a full, eventful life inside prison. She corresponds with people, calls friends collect on the prison phones. She orders presents from catalogs and has them sent to relatives. Somehow she sends money to her mother and younger siblings. Fay has an avid interest in AIDS and its impact on her fellow prisoners. She comforts other inmates. To ease the crippling loneliness of prison, she performs yoga and other self-help exercises.

Despite our shaky start, Fay eventually came to trust us. As tenuous as our initial relationship was, it is now firm and sustaining. When Lorie Savel was pregnant, Fay sent maternity presents. She continues to write me the most intimate, funny, and bizarre letters, a hilarious and poignant diary of her day-to-day struggles. She adds

chapters to her "autobiography" all the time. We receive her annotated prison records; her notes in the margins are always critical of prison bureaucracy. LaFonda Fay Foster is one of the most interesting people I've ever met. She is a good person who committed horrific crimes. Seeing her tears in that cell, I submerge myself in her pain. Then I envisage her five victims and I am torn. Yes, people on death row are there because they committed vicious crimes—though certainly race, class, and bad luck play too large a part in the outcomes of most capital cases. My camera only chronicles the repetitions of our injustice and hypocrisy. We can bury these people, but as long as these photographs exist, never will we bury the memories.

I received this note in the mail recently.

The Dream . . .

Translating a dream into reality takes great courage. Doubt is a constant enemy. When doubt reigns, there is a strong temptation to let go of part of the dream as a way of resolving inevitable tensions. Success depends on the ability to remain enthusiastic, focused and purposeful to the end.
—Author Unknown

Lou, Lorie and Courtney, just a note to let you know I'm thinking of you all.

Fay

WALTER LEE CARUTHERS

Nº B212

Riverbend Maximum Security Institution
Nashville, Tennessee

Year of birth   1946
Marital status   married
Children   two
Date of offense   October 11, 1980
Sentenced to death   February 8, 1983
Status   under appeal

Walter Lee Caruthers was convicted of first-degree murder, assault with intent to commit murder, two counts of aggravated kidnapping, and two charges of armed robbery. A codefendant, Reginald Watkins, was acquitted of the murder but convicted of all remaining charges and sentenced to life imprisonment. Their victims were twenty-two-year-old Wilhelmina Stahl and her eighteen-year-old brother George. The Stahls were hitchhiking from New York to Georgia when Caruthers and Watkins picked them up in Ohio and offered to drive them as far south as Knoxville.

In Knoxville, Caruthers and Watkins drove the Stahls to a vacant lot, where they revealed they intended to rob them. They ordered the Stahls to get into the trunk of the car and drove them to a secluded area. There they raped Wilhelmina, then took her to a nearby lake and drowned her. They stabbed George, shot him, and left him for dead. He survived to testify at their trials, where each man blamed the other for the homicide.

Source: *State v Caruthers*, 676 SW2d 935 (1984).

My journey to death row is my way of facing real and imagined demons. By confronting murderers—perpetrators of the most morally reprehensible act—I have reached a new understanding of the culture in which we live. The subject is difficult; it is tempting to look the other way. I allow the prisoners to speak for themselves, but the photographs are *my* voice. I hope that in them there is some truth for us all.

There is an axiom in the photography business: on location, nothing is ever as it should be. As I entered one of the maximum-security pods that house death-row prisoners in Tennessee, Walter Caruthers was mopping the floors. We paid little attention as Caruthers complained that we were scuffing his highly polished floor.

My studio had been in lengthy communication with another man on this death row, and we had come to see him. But at the last moment, he refused to sign the state's release form. Noticing our disappointment, the guard suggested that we ask Walter Caruthers if we could photograph him. After a couple of minutes of negotiation, Caruthers agreed. We couldn't believe that finding a replacement would be so easy.

Walter cleans seven days a week; that's his job. It allows him to spend most of his days outside his cell. He described the dynamics of the arrangement:

Over here they got it segregated. You got A, B, C, and D. And A is the max and then we're all of us maxed but, I mean, they've got a level program over here. See, I get to run around with no handcuffs on me. We got people that got to have handcuffs on them and then you got some that have to have leg irons on them. . . .

This is the latest system: maximum-security, single-level housing of small groups of prisoners, with the electric chair in the middle.

Some of the inmates we met were conflicted about their futures. Most either professed their innocence and were trying to rectify the injustice, or were in various ways preparing themselves for the inevitable. Walter seemed unruffled; he had a particular equilibrium and didn't worry about tomorrow. His philosophy was unique.

It's how you adjust your mind. You can adjust your mind to anything. . . . You can adjust your mind to being rich. You can adjust your mind to being poor. In this situation, it's all you do. Some people can't stand it. Right now, we've got some people that just can't stand the pressure.

Walter was under the impression that he would someday get off death row, even leave prison. He claimed he would not make any kind of deal in exchange for a mandatory life term. With his new lawyer, with time served and time off for good behavior, he would be out in a few years. I don't know if this is an illusion, but I'm skeptical. He also dispelled the myth that life on death row is intolerable. He claimed it wasn't that bad; even the food was okay.

I'm content. Now that may sound crazy but I can deal with these day-to-day. . . . I know exactly what's going to take place. I know what I got to do.

I had heard about people who preferred the regimented life of a soldier, mental patient, or prisoner. The fact that their decisions were made for them represented a certain kind of security. But it was obvious to me that Walter had paid a price for his tranquility. He looked tired. His baseball cap looked tired; the way he wore it backward, it seemed his alter ego. He didn't appear depressed, but now and then he drifted off the end of his sentences.

Everybody develops ways to cope with bad situations. My theory is that Walter gave up some part of himself to make prison tolerable. He nonetheless seems to be looking toward his future.

PHILIP WORKMAN

Nᵒ 95920

Riverbend Maximum Security Institution
Nashville, Tennessee

Year of birth	1953
Marital status	married while on death row
Children	one
Date of offense	August 5, 1981
Sentenced to death	March 30, 1982
Status	under appeal

The murder that sent Philip Workman to death row occurred in a Wendy's restaurant in Memphis in 1981. The state alleged that Workman entered the restaurant just before closing time, ordered, and ate slowly until the restaurant closed. Then, brandishing a gun, he ordered the employees into the manager's office, demanded the day's receipts, and taking an employee's car keys, locked the office and left. Unknown to Workman, however, one of the employees had tripped a silent alarm. As Workman left the restaurant, he encountered Lieutenant Ronald Oliver of the Memphis police. In the ensuing scuffle, Workman shot and killed Oliver and wounded another police officer. An hour later he was found hiding in some underbrush near the restaurant. At trial Workman admitted his role in the crime, claiming he was under the influence of drugs.

Source: *State v Workman*, 667 SW2d 44 (1984); United Press International, 9 February 1986; 14 August 1981; 7 August 1981.

The sad truth about capital punishment is, those without the capital get the punishment.

Philip Workman's comment set the mood for the rest of our interview. Thirty-nine at the time of our meeting in July 1992, Workman was the prototypical convict, complete with tattoos and bandanna. "I need a little color in my life," he explained. He was straight out of central casting. Workman wore prison-issue denim, with the prison name big and bold on the pants legs.

In the South, the juxtaposition of conservative values with economic progress produces a particular brand of morality. While in prison, Philip had found Jesus. In fact, he looked a little like the popular image of Jesus: long hair, mustache, and goatee. He had obviously cultivated the look, and somehow it worked.

Though he had had a tumultuous youth, his newfound religion seemed to have calmed him down. Tempered by the eleven years he had spent on death row, he had found a new language to express himself. It sounded familiar to us. Many occupants of "the last cells on the corridors" embrace some form of religion; there is no shortage of converts in prison.

Now and then Philip talked about the more macabre aspects of his sentence:

Each walk had like thirteen cells. . . . My cell was twelve cell . . . on three walk. And twelve cell on four walk was where the electric chair was. So like if I ever tried to escape and drilled through the wall, I'd just wind up in the electric chair room. . . . I used to think about that sometimes. The first years I didn't even know it but where I laid my head every night over there. . . . I slept for eight and a half years about four feet from the electric chair.

Although he meant the story to be humorous, he seemed truly tortured by the proximity of the instrument of death. For Philip, death row is an earthbound purgatory.

Workman had married since his conviction—the first of many inmates we were to meet who performed the ceremony inside the walls. He had answered a personal ad placed by a single white female seeking a Christian man. Philip figured nothing disqualified him from meeting that description. He now sees his wife six hours a week.

Later Philip placed his own ad, and through it he found a second champion—a woman who is helping him to raise money from religious groups to pay for his appeals. Philip recognizes that he may die in prison, but he wants to go down fighting, with competent representation.

I found myself thinking about his life and ambitions. It must be awful to live knowing exactly what your days and nights will be like, every day, every month, every year, eventually knowing even the hour your life will end. The penal system removes the mystery from life; perhaps that is the essence of punishment. This concept is probably too abstract to appreciate unless you've experienced the degrading routine of prison. Though I probably never will, I can at least dissect it with someone who has—I can come a little closer than many and get beyond the purely theoretical. It is this personal contact that has most affected my notions of prisons in general and the death penalty in particular.

Would I enter this prison to photograph Workman if he were not on death row, if he had not been accused of murder? Probably not. But this seems a good way to examine danger and aggression, explore the dark places inside each of us. Like most so-called experts, I fear the root of violence within myself; instead, I investigate it through those who have stepped over the line.

Philip claims that he and perhaps a third of the people in jail with him are innocent. This is an astonishing statement, of which I am wary. Maybe what he means is that many of the criminals known to law officers cannot be caught red-handed. But the system encourages getting trouble-makers off the streets, one way or the other. Most prisoners are guilty of something, even if they are not guilty as charged.

We talked about the fact that nobody in Tennessee has been executed in years. Philip felt no safer for it.

That's just a deception. . . . The only reason why there hasn't been an execution here's because nobody's appeals has finally run out yet.

Because it was Christmas, I included a decorated tree in several of Workman's portraits. The festive decorations seemed out of place. How could there be Christmas in a place like this? Eventually I went back to my K Mart–size studio, and Philip went back to a cell the size of a mattress. He had a room with a view.

We have windows. As far as I'm concerned, they can block mine up though because when I look out my window all I see is the door that goes into the execution room over there. So, you know. I don't look out my window a whole lot.

Olen "Eddie" Hutchison

№ 144432

Riverbend Maximum Security Institution
Nashville, Tennessee

Year of birth	1954
Marital status	single
Children	unknown
Date of offense	August 14, 1988
Sentenced to death	January 18, 1991
Status	under appeal

Olen Hutchison and several codefendants were convicted of conspiring to murder Hugh Huddleston for the proceeds of two large life insurance policies, of which Hutchison and a codefendant were beneficiaries. Huddleston had gone fishing in a pontoon boat, and had drowned in the presence of two of the accused. Though the medical examiner originally reported that the death appeared accidental, and Hutchison was apparently not at the scene, he was condemned to death.

Source: "Statement of Case" (fifteen-page draft) prepared by Mr. Hutchison's attorneys and sent to us by Mr. Hutchison. At the end of 1995, no appellate court had reviewed the case.

Not so long ago, dime-store mysteries told tales of love and lust, greed and malevolence. The fantasies were entertaining, but they were too dramatic to be realistic. But sometimes life mimics art. The charges against Olen "Eddie" Hutchison were conspiracy and first-degree murder. By his own admission, Olen did a little loan sharking. And by coincidence, the only person on whom he ever took out an insurance policy died of suspicious causes. He was at home in bed at the time of the murder.

From the time Olen was very young, he had worked. Extremely industrious, he had bought his own home by the time he was seventeen. An unlikely murderer, he claims he has no idea why he is facing the death penalty, even why he is in jail. This is the first conviction of Olen's life, and the state's case was circumstantial. Because Olen has plenty of money saved from his jobs and extracurricular businesses, he can afford to pursue his defense aggressively.

When I found out I was gonna be indicted, I transferred everything out of my name . . . and still, I live comfortably. . . . I don't hurt. A lot of these guys don't have nothing. And the only thing I have to be careful about is how much money comes in here and how much goes out. Because then they'd start trying to tax me on it.

We exchanged many letters with Olen before finally establishing our credibility. He then sent us volumes of trial transcripts and other materials. The transcripts were quite useful; in this case the facts were complicated. But Olen's claim was simple, though not very comprehensible when put in his own words.

See, anytime, anytime you are found guilty of first-degree murder and the corpus delicti says hey, there's got to be a crime committed. Here we started with no crime and they made a crime. See, they just turned it around. So there, my issue, the corpus delicti issue, hasn't been met. Just because you have the dead body don't mean that it's been murdered.

We were pretty clandestine about this project, not telling our friends and relatives what we were doing. We really didn't know how to proceed, and we were a little paranoid as well. Traveling around, we became habitués of truck stops in penitentiary towns. The colorful nightlife, the country music, the beer: it was all kind of sleazy and in its own way relaxing.

Come morning, it's another story. Death row is tense in Nashville, and security is high, albeit invisible. Not many people could be seen in common areas. The high-tech design of the pods where inmates are housed has reduced the number of personnel needed to manage the ever-increasing numbers held in the prison.

The room where we took the photographs had an odd shape, designed that way for a reason. Using convex mirrors, one guard outside the room could see every nook and cranny and monitor all activ-

ity inside the visiting space. Mirrors were everywhere. I thought they might be used to suggest the "fishbowl" atmosphere of prison. Reflected in a mirror, Olen's image is a story within a story. It reminds me of the climactic scene in Orson Welles's film *Lady from Shanghai:* you don't know where to look, what is real and what is imagined.

I was so anxious to get an image on film, I went to work in a panic, without thinking—afraid the authorities would rescind their permission at any moment. I heard hardly a word Hutchison was saying, so I wrote my description of him with the aid of my photographs and recordings. Olen is feline in appearance and nature—not like a domesticated house cat, but a lion or a tiger. He talked about his situation in a conspiratorial manner, curling around his chair, careful not to say anything incriminating. Nothing in Olen's background could make us believe he was capable of what he was charged with. Mired in a case of murder by proxy, he was not violent, but litigious. He knew how to use the court system to his advantage.

Because I'm . . . I'm suit happy. Do something to me, I'm gonna sue you. You want to give me that right, I'm gonna do it. And I figure that everybody's like I am.

Prison is changing Eddie's white-collar attitude, though. Prison is fertile ground for all kinds of education, and now Olen is learning a darker side.

Well, there's a lot of things I didn't know when I came to prison. I didn't know how to hot-wire a car. I didn't know how to do forgery. I didn't know how to manipulate the law. . . .

How to build bombs. You learn all the bad stuff. . . . Prison does not rehabilitate.

Proponents of the death penalty say, "An eye for an eye," or "Let the punishment fit the crime." That may sound good in theory, but no one believes that every person convicted of murder should die. We are therefore faced with the problem of determining who should live and who should die. All human history tells us that we are not good at making such decisions. As Justice Harry Blackmun said shortly before his retirement from the Supreme Court:

I am . . . optimistic . . . that this Court eventually will conclude that the effort to eliminate arbitrariness while preserving fairness in the infliction of death is so plainly doomed to failure that it—and the death penalty—must be abandoned altogether. I may not live to see that day, but I have faith that eventually it will arrive. The path the Court has taken lessens us all.[1]

[1]*Callins v Collins*, 22 February 1994.

GARY GRAHAM

Nᵒ 696

Ellis I Unit   Huntsville, Texas

Year of birth	1963
Marital status	single
Children	two
Date of offense	May 13, 1981
Sentenced to death	October 28, 1981
Status	under appeal

Gary Graham was sent to death row for shooting Bobby Grant Lambert in a grocery-store parking lot at the age of seventeen. Graham, who committed nine aggravated robberies in May 1981, was arrested after falling asleep in the course of a robbery and rape. At least one other of his victims was shot, though not fatally; several of his crimes involved guns and the threat of violence.

From the start Graham admitted to the robberies, but he has steadfastly denied involvement in Lambert's murder. The chief evidence against him came from the eyewitness testimony of Bernadine Skillern, an African-American elementary school clerk who had witnessed the shooting, chased the suspect, and fingered him despite her opposition to the death penalty. To this day Skillern stands by her identification. Little was done at trial to undermine the effect of her testimony.

Then in 1988, four witnesses came forward to say that Graham had been with them on the night the murder occurred. Other holes in the state's case were found and challenged. In 1993 Graham began to correspond with a woman in California, who publicized his case and enlisted the support of a number of celebrities. His age, his race, and the possibility that he was railroaded at trial have postponed Graham's execution several times. At this writing in 1995, his fate was undecided.

Source: *Graham v Collins*, 829 FSupp. 204 (1993); *National Law Journal*, 16 May 1994; *Los Angeles Times*, 7 September 1993.

Early in 1993, at a point where we were stymied and making no progress, I received a call from the Texas Resource Center (a federally funded organization that until 1995 assisted attorneys who handle death-penalty appeals in Texas). A man was to be executed seven days hence. Gary Graham was known to us through a referral from Lisa Radelet, but we had not been able to get in touch with him—a common occurrence in Texas. Graham's attorneys had found witnesses for his alibi, to corroborate his claim that he was not the perpetrator. The Resource Center had heard of our project, and wanted me to photograph their client to support their final pleas to the pardons board and Governor Ann Richards.

The request was one I wanted to accommodate, but I didn't know how. I had been trying to get into Texas prisons for a long time, but to no avail. In fact, I had requested permission to visit six other inmates, and was hoping to go down for two days and photograph as many of them as time would permit—a tall order for any death row, but especially the black hole of Texas. Though the Resource Center recognized the value of my work, it had no special access to Texas prisons and no idea how to help us.

Texas death row is one of the most restricted in the country. All visitations must occur in a specially designated part of the common area. Inmates are required to be in a cage, separated from visitors by wire mesh. No exceptions. No photographs. "Media visitations" are allowed only on Wednesdays, under the same restrictions. There is no privacy.

Of course, I had other ideas. I wanted to meet each inmate individually, with no glass, wire, or other restraints between us. I had just three days to make it happen: the Friday prior to the execution date was my only window of opportunity.

To reach my objective I had to solve problems on several fronts simultaneously. I decided to play my trump card: I asked a few influential politicians to make some phone calls. Eventually Lorie Savel was able to negotiate with officials at the Texas Department of Corrections, and we were given permission to photograph Graham without glass, handcuffs, or guards. We could return two

weeks later to photograph the other six men, and we could have two days to do it.

(I still don't know how Lorie got those doors to open.)

Getting through those doors may not have been easy, but the approval had come from so high up that our actual entrance was relatively simple. But I knew as soon as I entered, I was in a house of madness. Chaos seemed to reign. People were scurrying everywhere. Huge guards orbited us, trying to block our vision.

Gary Graham had a history of rebelling against his jailers; he had been a dangerous juvenile when he was arrested. Totally out of control then, he has now accepted the fact that he may become a martyr in a fight to abolish the death penalty.

But most of the people that I deal with, they realize that we are basically fighting a war here. And, unfortunately, in wars you are going to have casualties. And we all recognize that we may . . . I may be a casualty of the system. . . .

By the time we met him, Gary had been protesting his innocence for twelve years. He had even had to argue with his current lawyer, to convince him that his innocence should be used as his defense.

And when he got on the case, his main . . . we had a big fight because his main concern was dealing with the mitigation issue. And I'm saying, "I'm innocent. Let's work on the innocent question." But he didn't have much faith in that. And I could tell that in dealing with him. . . . So I had to fight with him. And we had some serious fights. And eventually he began to piece by piece go back and look at the puzzle and investigate the puzzle and was able to uncover substantial evidence proving my innocence that we're really working on right now.

But Gary's case illustrates the principle that innocence is no defense. That is to say, fourteen years after his conviction, the question of his innocence is subordinate to legal procedure. Under Texas law, appeals are limited; if evidence is brought to light too late, an innocent prisoner can be executed under the statute of limitations.

Though race and social class affect who is sentenced to death, probably the most significant factor is inadequate legal defense at trial. That was certainly the case for Gary Graham. Witnesses who could verify that Gary was not the murderer were never called to testify. Like the majority of criminals who are subject to the death penalty, he was unable to pay for adequate legal representation, so the court appointed his lawyer. Because a court-appointed defense is often substandard and underfinanced, death sentences are frequently overturned on appeal. Nearly a third of those sentenced to death in the United States over the last two decades have had their sentences reduced to a prison term.

Gary Graham's case has become an international cause célèbre. How did a poor juvenile offender become the concern of movie stars, ministers, and civic leaders? Danny Glover, Kenny Rogers, and Willie Nelson have become personally involved in his case; songs have been written about him.

I think it is because the most egregious error a society could make is to incarcerate and kill an innocent man. Though it is inconceivable that our supposed fail-safe system could deprive an innocent person of his freedom, much less his life, irrevocable evidence exists that it has done so hundreds of times. (See Michael L. Radelet, Hugo Adam Bedau, and Constance E. Putnam, *In Spite of Innocence* [Boston: Northeastern University Press, 1992].) Since 1970, sixty people have been released from death row because of evidence of their innocence. I have personally met several people who have been sentenced to death and are now free.

In this case, I was talking to such a man just days before his scheduled death. I was nervous about treading on sacred ground. Did we have any right to be with him during his final days? But Gary had rehearsed the end of his life so many times, he was unfazed. Though his voice showed years of pent-up hostility, I thought I should hear more rage in it; I anticipated more adrenaline. My own anger was incandescent. Despite his burden, he remained calm and deliberate as I tentatively worked around him, making exposures. He was in charge of his emotions; it shows in the photographs.

Days later Gary received a stay of his execution. His case continues to perplex the appellate courts.

JAMES LEE BEATHARD

Nº 785

Ellis I Unit   Huntsville, Texas

Year of birth	1957
Marital status	divorced prior to sentencing
Children	two
Date of offense	October 9, 1984
Sentenced to death	March 5, 1985
Status	under appeal

James Lee Beathard was convicted of killing Marcus Hathorn, a fourteen-year-old boy, and the boy's parents, Gene and Linda Sue Hathorn. The Hathorns' elder son, Gene, Jr. ("Geno"), was also convicted. The Hathorns were murdered by shotgun in their trailer home in Rusk, Texas. The state argued that Hathorn and Beathard had committed the murders so Geno could inherit his parents' $150,000 estate—although it turned out Geno's name had been removed from their will. To give the appearance that the family had been murdered by drug-crazed burglars, the two men stole items from the Hathorns' home and planted false evidence.

In an attempt to escape the death sentence, Geno confessed to the murders against his attorney's advice. At Beathard's trial he testified that he had hired Beathard to kill his family for $12,500. In

1985 Geno's testimony was used to convict him; he received the death sentence. (He later recanted his testimony.) Though Beathard admitted he was at the scene of the crime, he claimed he had gone expecting only to make some quick cash in a drug deal. Geno, he claimed, had committed the crime without his knowledge.

Source: *Hathorn v State*, 848 SW2d 101 (1992); *Beathard v State*, 767 SW2d 423 (1989); United Press International, 28 October 1992, 8 March 1989, 6 March 1985.

Texas takes great pride in being the United States' leading executioner. In Huntsville, where the executions are performed, the Chamber of Commerce advertises the state's original electric chair, "Old Sparky," as a tourist attraction. Over four hundred people currently inhabit the two death rows—a small one for women and an enormous one for men. Given the size and notoriety of the one in Huntsville, I had hoped from the beginning of the project for the opportunity to visit it. We wrote several letters, and eventually six death-row inmates agreed to be photographed.

Before I met with James Beathard, I received three very detailed letters expressing his interest in the project. Not sure whether I could capture the essence of death row, he argued that if I was to succeed, I would need to spend sufficient time on the unit for an extended photo-essay. In a letter dated February 28, 1993, he wrote:

That's where we really look no different from everybody in the outside world, except for the white clothes and the "rundown factory," bleak setting. . . . The relaxed smiles, the joking and the camaraderie, that's when we're truly ourselves. When you see someone playing "air guitar" to the radio in their cell, or "high-fiving" during a football or basketball game in the day room, we're pretty much like anybody else. . . . There are the looks of pained resignation when we have to wear the shackles, cuffs and chains whenever we have to leave the unit. . . .

In a return letter, we tried to explain that the Texas Department of Corrections (TDC) called the shots. Though we were requesting free rein, unrestricted passage through the unit might be more than we could expect.

Beathard's letters expressed what appeared to be genuine appreciation and enthusiasm for photography. He reported that he had attempted to shoot several photo-essays himself. He wrote at length about a project he had imagined but would probably never realize, a study of the stone chimneys and fireplaces of old Texas homesteads, now abandoned and overgrown. Beathard sees them as the only remaining monuments to the families whose lives were lived around them.

Beathard's letters contradicted the grim picture the press had painted of him. Once I had met him, I decided his correspondence gave the more accurate portrayal. James Lee Beathard walked into the room with a happy-go-lucky manner and the voice and animation of a disc jockey. Big and burly, he reminded me of an old-fashioned neighborhood filling-station attendant. You could stop to talk to him, forget what you had to do, and pass more time than you had to spare. Articulate and well-spoken, Beathard was extremely frank.

There's a general image of what a prison convict is. You know, uneducated, crude, uncaring, tough, hard-nosed bastard, you know. . . . There's this unspoken assumption that people doing five years and people doing ten years— the man doing ten years is probably twice as bad as the one doing five years. The man doing the thirty-year hitch is probably six times as bad as the man doing five years. And the guy doing the—facing the death penalty—is like the worst-possible imaginable extreme you can ever come up with.

Inside the TDC, the towering walls bleed the sweat of confinement and echo with the prisoners' shouts. Here, more than in any other prison, I felt the weight of souls just marking time. As Beathard wrote in a letter dated March 5, 1995:

This place, all prisons are factories for grinding the human soul into blood and pain, with fear and loathing as the end product.

No matter where we went, we were obliged to walk down the center of the hall, while the trustees walked next to the walls. The prison is an overcrowded city, with people in every nook and cranny. Visitors are outsiders; we are the only ones who can really walk away from this. The truth is

that no one else can: not prisoners, not guards, not families, and certainly not victims.

We asked Beathard why he was there, a question meant both literally and philosophically. Beathard answered literally.

The problem is I'm involved in a situation where another person committed murder. That he tried to make a deal for himself and he tied me into murders. I had no idea the murders were going to happen. That got me down here. Since I've been down here, the laws have changed so that even if you don't know the murder's going to happen, you didn't directly participate in it, you can still be held under death penalty for it. . . . I feel stupid even saying, "I didn't do it." Because everybody says that.

Prior to his conviction, Beathard had worked at the state hospital in Rusk, a licensed substance-abuse counselor. While he was there he had met a death-row inmate, David Powell, who had come to the hospital for an evaluation (see page 65). Beathard had had an opportunity to speak with Powell and observe how people can become so estranged and alienated, they veer off into a totally different kind of life. Through David, he could see how otherwise good people can get caught in unforeseen circumstances that shape their destiny. Ironically, Beathard and Powell now must spend the rest of their lives together.

If somebody would have told me in '78 that in 1988 I'd be his cell partner—this on death row. I mean, that would have been just too weird to even think about. . . . It was something that just stabbed me in the heart.

I take most of my pictures in prisons in very small, sterile rooms. To take advantage of the environment and incorporate some distinguishing icons, I spread out my equipment, spilling out into the halls. I stepped outside the cell to photograph Beathard through the window, alone with Lorie Savel. All I could see were hands gesticulating in the air; TV without sound.

Beathard is a leader on death row. He is editor of the jailhouse publication *Texas Death Row Journal*, a periodical that has the tacit approval of the TDC. The *Journal* is a service-oriented newsletter that goes to interested parties outside the prison.

You know, the *Journal* will always be open to the victims [victims' families] if they want to write. We really would like to get them involved. . . . What would you like to see done? What would help you get on with your life?

Beathard regrets the loss of lifelong friends who said they believed he was innocent, but nonetheless severed their connections with him. He had grown up with several of them, even risked his life for some, and their abandonment cut him deeply. Since he came to prison, his new friendships have transcended the old ones.

There was a guy here who died recently. He had an excellent sense of humor. . . . And after somebody gets executed, after the fact, they have like a moment of silence. Which is cool. . . . But Red used to hate that moment of silence. . . . And about five years ago, there was a Monty Python skit. . . . They come out dressed in barbershop quartet and they sing this really rude ditty. . . .

Anyway, during one of these moments of silence, Red said, "Man if they ever do that," he says, "you've got to mess that up for me. . . . Tell a joke or something."

Well, they got him a few months ago. . . . So they had their little moment of silence. I jumped up on a big table out there and I—I did my best full-fledged barbershop quartet. . . . But I told 'em, I said, "That's for Red, that's what he wanted."

Beathard mourned other losses—his children and friends—and fantasized about freedom.

Personally I'd like to build me a decent motorcycle, tour the country, just go on a long bike trip—a road trip from hell, so to speak—catch a freighter across to Europe, check out Ireland and England, maybe north coast of Europe, come back here, find me a nice lady, get a couple of kids, settle down and just do my thing.

It costs a lot of money to execute people. Convicts are stacking up on death rows, in part because of the high cost of appointing attorneys to fight their appeals. In some counties prosecutors no longer seek the death sentence because capital trials are so expensive. In his ten years on death row, Beathard has considered the exorbitant cost as only a death-row inmate can.

The death penalty just doesn't hurt us. . . . For every person that gets executed the state spends about $2 million, from beginning to end. So 350 people represent $700 million. . . . Guess who loses? Women, Infants, and Children . . . that's WIC. . . . I'm worth $2 million. And they're basically taking money out of . . . food out of the mouths of children to kill me. . . . They could lock me up forever for $800,000 or less. . . . I said, "Look, I don't care if I didn't do it or not. Kill me please and just put the money in the WIC or somewhere else. I'll drop the appeal."

The list of writers who are convicted felons is long and illustrious: Herman Melville, O. Henry, Jack London, Malcolm X. Beathard may not be in the same class, but when each new issue of his newspaper comes out, I read it cover to cover.

ROBERT WEST

Nº 731

Ellis I Unit   Huntsville, Texas

Year of birth	1961
Marital status	single
Children	none
Date of offense	August 24, 1982
Sentenced to death	January 11, 1983
Status	under appeal

Robert West was convicted of killing DeAnn Klaus in a drunken rage in 1982. Both lived at the Memorial Park Motel in Houston, where Klaus worked in the bar. Police reports indicate that West broke into Klaus's room, tied her to the bed with fishing twine, and strangled and stabbed her. Residents of the motel saw West leave the victim's room covered with blood and called the police; shortly after West was arrested.

According to West, the victim's boyfriend had killed his brother by mistake, intending to kill him. In retaliation, West killed Klaus. All four knew each other and were involved in drug dealing.

Source: *West v State*, 720 SW2d 511 (1986); United Press International, 11 July 1987, 26 May 1987, 24 August 1982.

On death row, just when you think you can drop your guard, you are reminded that madmen inhabit prisons—on both sides of the iron bars. We had been inside Ellis I for hours. We had interviewed half a dozen denizens, and had begun to feel comfortable. Suddenly, the guards indicated they could no longer guarantee our safety. But we smugly felt we could handle any jailhouse encounter. When Robert West was escorted in, we were made aware of our own arrogance.

In appearance, West is probably the most stereotypical criminal I have met: a skinhead haircut and numerous tattoos, and a face that's a conspiracy. There was something going on behind those eyes. Trouble. Sean Penn would have played him in a movie.[1]

Most prisoners who have spent years in confinement are docile, but West's manner was all flint and cinders. Steam seemed to rise from his shoulders. Standing five feet, nine inches, he seemed larger than life. West had known freedom for just two years since the age of thirteen; he was the quintessential recidivist, the reason prisons are built. We introduced ourselves, and I reached out to shake hands. He radiated attitude.

This is my third time in the penitentiary. I told them, "All right, you think I'm too young to be in prison so I'll show you what a youngster

[1]Prior to this book's printing we learned that director Tim Robbins had chosen Penn to play the condemned prisoner in the movie version of Sister Helen Prejean's book *Dead Man Walking*: a coincidence.

does in prison." So, for six years I went on a rampage, throwing feces and urine on every guard that walked by my cell. Every opportunity I got, I came out of my cell and jumped on him. We were fighting. We were tearing stuff up. Tore all the TVs off the wall. Tore the toilets and sinks off the wall. I lived in solitary for the entire summer of 1985.

West spent a good portion of the interview trying to get a reaction from Lorie Savel by being extremely graphic about his life in prison.

Back then we used to have this medication here called Artane. It's a muscle-relaxer that they give the people that are on Thorazine and stuff. It's a good drug. . . . We'd go down and see the shrink and get him to put us on Thorazine to get the Artane . . . and we'd throw the Thorazine in the toilet and do the Artane. The problem with that was . . . it made you take a shit when you took it. . . . Anyway I tore my toilet off the wall after doing the Artane and I hadn't taken a shit yet, so I was in trouble. . . . They finally came in with the SORT team and they cut my door off with a blowtorch. They got tear-gas canisters pointing in there. He [a guard] come running in with all seven of them pushing him. He was like a kamikaze. They projected him in there. . . . He came in and I caught one of them in the face and then got punched and then flipped over on the bed and then that big motherfucker put his knee in the small of my back and put all that weight on it. . . . I shit in my drawers because of the Artane. Then they beat. They beat. They beat the handcuffs. They beat the shackles on and took me up out of the cell.

When I planned this project it had always been my intention to take a woman with me into the prisons. Interviews and portrait sessions can be tricky, even with the most cooperative subjects. I knew I would be given only one chance, and I thought a woman's presence might improve the odds. Women humanize most situations, and Lorie has a special talent for drawing people out.

Though West tested Lorie often, the rapport that developed between them was palpable.

This is the first time in ten years that I've sat with anybody outside of the system. It's kind of uncomfortable to tell you the truth because I haven't been in this kind of situation and don't know how to react and I keep—sometimes in my head—like sitting here looking at you, I'm kind of reverting back to the free world again— like this is a normal thing. And I have to re- mind myself there are just some parts of you that you have to leave behind and that you can't carry in here no more. You just can't be a whole human. You have to set it aside.

Robert's cigarette smoke rings filled the room. He wasn't supposed to smoke but somehow it re- placed the steam. Lorie was able to get West to talk about his harsh childhood.

I was born in Jacksonville, Florida, and adopted by my grandparents when I was six months old and raised in Rockford, Illinois, thirty-six miles southwest of Chicago. And I went to reform school and after I got out, went back to Florida. I was on the quest to find my father and mother and I found her and we didn't get along. We were too much the same. We both ran from our problems. We were like magnets that won't come together. Just keep pushing each other apart.

The abandonment by his parents scarred him for life. His reunion with his mother was misguided; his relationship with her was a psychological minefield. She could give him no answers. His confusion was revealing and unnerving.

She was fifteen years old when she had me. When I got out of reform school, the first time I met her I was eighteen years old. She was thirty-four years old when I met her. The first thing she said to me was, "You got a joint?" So we're sitting there and we're smoking a joint and we're drinking a beer and I don't see her as mother no more. . . . And we sat around smoking a joint and we partied and we had the same kind of relationship you have with a lover except there was no sex and no conversation of it. . . . And I was thinking about it. "This ain't my mother. I don't know this woman." I told her what I was really thinking and probably why I didn't get as close to her as I could have because those were the thoughts that I was having. I don't know if they was right or wrong. I still don't.

Prison and reform school were his parents. Such an upbringing is bound to give a distorted sense of the world.

Even the little time West spent out of jail had been a problem for him.

I wanted whatever I wanted. I was spoiled like that because everything was easy. Everything was too easy. I played baseball. They wanted me to go to school and do the work. I did that and knocked it out fast. It was easy. It was simple. In white upper-middle-class America, it was like the American dream. Everything was perfect, except the things that I started seeing there.

In prison, West seemed to thrive on the conflict he created. The visions he conjured up were bloodcurdling.

They brought in this squad they called the SORT team, Special Operations Response Team. They were torturers. They came in. Eight of them in a cell on a person; bend his fingers, twist his toes, pressure points here, pulling hair, stretching your mouth open, squeezing your nuts, carrying you down the hall naked while they're squeezing your nuts and twisting all those things. . . . They taught them how to hurt without leaving bruises and internal injuries.

At his most recalcitrant, West was thrown into solitary confinement.

For the entire summer of 1985, they turned the heat on, too, and cut the water off. You get this claustrophobic kind of feeling. Heat gets on you. Your mouth is drying. You want to do something to get away from this heat but you can't go nowhere. . . . You get those bursts of energy from inside and you want to run. You want to do something and you can't. You're trapped.

Though West has cultivated his reputation for trouble, the last couple of years have brought a complete reversal of his behavior (much like his attitude toward us changed entirely during our interview). He is one of those prisoners who got married on death row. He does not feud with his jailers anymore, and has calmed down in other ways. Volcanic in his youth, he seems to have matured. West was the editor of the prison publication, the *Endeavor*, a duty he shared with Gary Graham. He now passes his days writing—for publication, to friends and acquaintances—and reading.

In spite of the system, I went in another direction and started reading. I read Dostoyevsky, Tolstoy, Nietzsche, Camus. I don't appreciate Nietzsche, by the way. . . . I think Nietzsche is too blunt, too crude and I think he's supremist. . . . I'd rather see people take up Camus, Tolstoy, Dostoyevsky—more humanistic. Camus

really turned me on—"neither victims, nor executioners, nor rebels. . . ."

West's own story reads like a Greek tragedy: abandoned by his mother as a child, he killed the wrong person to avenge his brother's death.

Our extended stay in Texas had allowed us to meet an enormous range of personalities—a microcosm of what we were to find everywhere else. Because we were in and out of Ellis I several times, we got to know the guards there fairly well. As a courtesy, they allowed us to walk onto the Row. It struck me as a medieval dungeon: on a bright, hot summer day, it was pitch black inside. A cacophony of wails and expletives rose up as I entered. Small points of light flickered in the dark: little mirrors and reflective devices held through the bars at right angles, to show who might be invading. I took one tentative step and was ordered to stop. The guards, who used floor-to-ceiling shields when they ventured onto the cellblock themselves, would not allow me further.

Robert West's cell was at the end.

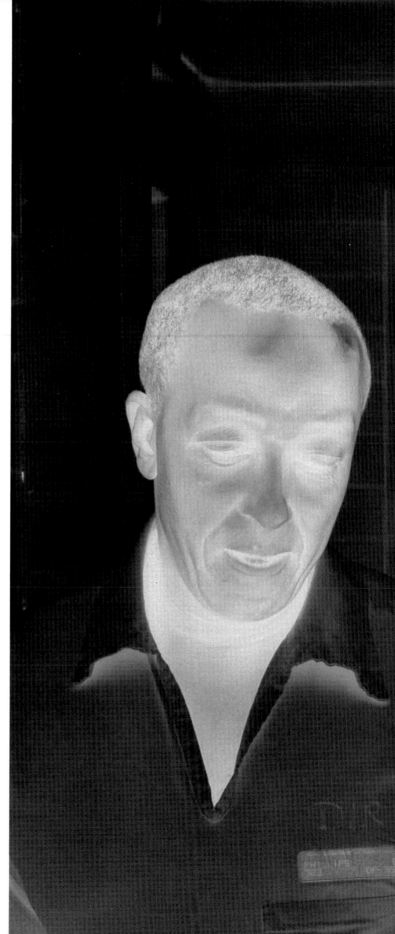

ABDULLAH BASHIR,
A.K.A. CLIFFORD PHILLIPS

Nº 723

Ellis I Unit Huntsville, Texas

Year of birth   1935

Marital status   married while on
                           death row

Children   two, by a previous
                           marriage

Date of offense   January 13, 1982

Sentenced to death   September 13, 1982

Status   executed December 15,
                           1993, by lethal injection

Abdullah Bashir was convicted of strangling Iris Siff, 58, during a robbery at the Alley Theater in Houston. Siff had been a performer and administrator at the theater for thirty years. She was working late the night of her death, filling out an application for a government grant. Bashir, a former security guard at the theater, had been fired a few weeks earlier for sleeping on the job. According to Bashir, he went to Siff's office to collect the back wages he felt were owed to him. During the ensuing argument, Bashir strangled Siff with a telephone cord. Arrested outside his mother's home in Los Angeles a month after the murder, he made a full confession. Like his victim, all the members of the jury that convicted him were white, and they took only forty minutes to agree on the death sentence.

Source: *Phillips v State*, 701 SW2d 875 (Tex Cr App 1985); *New York Times*, 16 December 1995; *Buffalo News*, 22 September 1993; United Press International, 16 October 1985, 14 September 1982, 9 August 1982.

I focused my camera. Staring back at me through the lens was a face dark as night, but full of harmony. Through the viewfinder, he reminded me of many of the men I knew growing up—vital men, straight and true. Yet in focus his uniform seemed to weigh him down. Abdullah Bashir's prison whites, crisp and starched, looked heavy and formal. His clothing contrasted starkly with his complexion and surroundings, but matched his unblemished demeanor perfectly. I could see the acceptance of fate in his face. Look closely at his photograph, framed by the doorway. In black and white, it tells all.

Bashir's manner recalled a time long gone. He spoke of his life on the outside, when he lived in New York as a family man. He had been a member of the board of his church, had worked on community projects, and had visited local prisons. He recalled several Moslem imams who had been influential in his life. He had a hundred stories, all ancient history. His existence on death row was his present. And that meant no future. His bearing was almost regal; his every utterance was crafted and thoughtful.

I haven't gotten to that point where I've given up on myself, you know. I still love life and if I didn't think that I was still a productive person then perhaps my attitude would be different, you know. But I could stay here another fifty years. . . . It wouldn't matter.

Bashir's spirituality, tinged with Middle Eastern mysticism, was very unlike the agnosticism of other death-row convicts we had met, like Ed Kennedy or Robert West. But it was clear as well that he had become a creature of habit. Habit had replaced happiness. Years of repeated routine had taken its toll. There was no drama left.

The Department of Corrections, including most of the guards, insisted on using Bashir's old "slave" name, which he had changed in 1974. He had done business, bought property, existed as Abdullah Bashir for years. Now he was Clifford Phillips again. How jarring is it to one's self-image to make such a drastic change? How insulting to have the courts, the police refuse to use one's chosen name?

We queried Bashir at length about his crime, why he thought he was on death row. My camera shutter and the strobe lights punctuated his words.

Spiritually I could just feel myself . . . I was like a man falling from a height down to a level and couldn't put on the brakes. And I just kept falling.

I woke up one morning here on death row. . . .

His philosophy seemed to be a pragmatism laced with a strange optimism.

I didn't feel bad once I got here. For some reason I felt I had an opportunity to really get my life together. And I think that was the most joyful experience . . . feeling I had when I come here. I didn't see death. I didn't see it perhaps the way people see it. A lot of people come here and see life coming to its final stages. I didn't see that. I seen something altogether different.

We pressed him further, and optimism evolved into spiritualism.

I just attribute my being here to being indifferent to some of my moral values, being disobedient, from being rebellious.

Bashir had constructed another reality, beginning a second life when he arrived on death row. He severed his ties with his past and substituted new relationships for old ones. He corresponded with a woman in Ireland whom he had never met. Eventually she emigrated and converted to Islam, and they were married. She visited Bashir regularly.

Though prison marriages are not infrequent, no scholar has ever investigated them. Why some prisoners marry is shrouded in mystery. We can assume that prisoners need contacts on the outside, for affection, for dignity, for survival; it's easier to do time when you have someone than when you're alone. Still, to vow to stay together "until death do us part" is more difficult to understand when the death has already been scheduled.

For most of us, death is sometime in the future. Twenty years, ten years—it's an abstraction. But time wears differently on a person who knows the scheduled hour. Bashir understood time in his own way, in the framework of his own reality. It had become very finite and he was calm in his expectations.

They're trying to speed up executions in the state of Texas. I'm sure you heard about that.

They won't settle for being second. They want to be the trailblazers when it comes to taking life. So they're not wasting no time.

Abdullah's life had been sculpted by big events: early incarceration, an identity change, murder, death row, marriage. This was not the life he'd envisioned but it would have to do.

Bashir had suffered through several stays of execution. We had been involved with one of his vigils ourselves, held our breath all day long. But though he was granted another last-minute stay, his reprieve was brief; he had been living on borrowed time. Five months after I photographed him, he was executed.

Bashir's execution shook me. Of all the inmates I had met, I thought he was the least likely to be executed. The first recorded execution in the United States occurred in 1608 in Jamestown, Virginia, by firing squad. The first man to be executed by lethal injection was Charles Brooks in Huntsville, Texas, on December 7, 1982. Abdullah Bashir, a.k.a. Clifford Phillips, was the seventy-first.

LESLEY LEE GOSCH

Nº 842

Ellis I Unit   Huntsville, Texas

Year of birth	1955
Marital status	single
Children	none
Date of offense	September 18, 1985
Sentenced to death	September 4, 1986
Status	under appeal

Lesley Lee Gosch, a former Eagle Scout, was convicted of killing the wife of a San Antonio bank president in a botched extortion attempt. He shot Rebecca Jo Patton in the head six times with a handgun. The key evidence against Gosch came from his partner in crime, John Laurence Rogers, who testified against him in exchange for a lighter sentence. Gosch's attorney later told the press that Rogers's testimony was given in retaliation for a statement Gosch made against Rogers in an earlier trial.

Source: *Gosch v State*, 829 SW2d 775 (1991); United Press International, 5 September 1986.

I was setting up my equipment when the guards led Lesley Gosch into the room that had been set aside for interviews. He stood silently for several moments before my crew realized he was in the room. Coke-bottle-thick lenses in prison-issue

frames drew attention to his eyes, giving him a gnomish appearance. He had lost one eye and the tips of his fingers in an accident, when a chemical used to make blasting caps exploded.

My vision is so bad that my right eye is . . . I lost it in 1977 and my left one, they've taken the lens out. That's why I wear these cataract glasses. I take my glasses off and I'm legally blind.

We joked about the lighter side of prison life. Gosch told a story about a practical joke that he played on one of the guards.

We had a new officer working the wing and . . . I was feeling particularly frustrated that day, so I took my eye out and put it in the carrots on my food tray and called him back over and said, "Look, I want another tray. I don't know where the rest of him is, but I ain't eat-ing this part of it." I've had a lot of fun with my prosthesis.

Despite this sense of humor, Lesley is a loner. On death row, activity is a matter of choice. Some have a social life; others seek invisibility.

Gosch has become something of an artist, teach-ing himself an intricate pointillist technique using pen and ink. Because of his failing eyesight, he works with his nose only an inch or two from the canvas.

I started drawing when I was in county jail. . . . They gave us a few pencils and pens and tablets. . . . The walls in my cell were made out of steel with enamel paint. You could draw on them with your pencils. So, I started drawing on the wall and went from there. And after I got down here, I got to where I could get a few art books and they allowed a whole-lot-greater variety of materials. And so I—you don't have anything else to do.

Trained as an electrical engineer at Texas A&M and the University of Texas at San Antonio, Gosch is a bright, well-educated man, with well-reasoned opinions on crime and punishment. Most interesting to me, though, were his ideas about art.

Art, for me, is a form of communication with a high path applied to it. Everybody communi-cates but the craftsmanship's in the com-munications—everybody can speak, but not everybody can speak in pictures . . . in some

form of high craft. It's been said, over the years, that art is to the highest craftsman. And it's true.

It must be difficult to come to art while in prison, to develop an aesthetic under such adverse conditions. Did Gosch take up the challenge or was it just a way of passing the time? Either way it must be an obsession, a kind of mental gymnastics that has the effect of keeping his mind off his surroundings and his ultimate fate. I was familiar with art for pleasure, art for profit, and art as politics, but this was a new category.

I guess it's just the pressure of not knowing. The fear it generates. You don't know what the outcome is going to be and you're just in constant limbo.

I had always thought that evil could be sensed; really bad people exuded it. But Gosch's countenance gave no hint of it. I don't know if the real man was hidden behind his large glasses, or if his aversion to the constant limbo of death row made him look harmless. In his manner and his way of speaking I sensed only his confusion and despair.

I have no doubt that the United States will ultimately reject the death penalty, that future generations will look back and wonder, "Who were those executioners? How could our ancestors have tolerated such irrational behavior?" The change will not come easily; the issue is extraordinarily complex. Democracy is hard.

DAVID LEE POWELL

Nº 612

Ellis I Unit   Huntsville, Texas

Year of birth	1951
Marital status	single
Children	none
Date of offense	May 18, 1978
Sentenced to death	September 11, 1978
Status	pending resentencing

David Lee Powell was convicted of killing a police officer in Austin in 1978. Ralph Ablanedo had confronted Powell and his girlfriend, Sheila Meinert, on a routine traffic stop. Who fired the AK-47 automatic rifle at him has never been clear. Meinert was sentenced to fifteen years in prison and released in 1989. At the time of the murder, Powell, a student at the University of Texas and a heavy drug user, pleaded insanity. In 1989 the Supreme Court reversed his conviction, but in 1991 Powell was resentenced in front of eighty-five uniformed police officers. The Texas Court of Criminal Appeals vacated the second death sentence in 1994; a new trial is pending.

Source: *Powell v State*, 742 SW2d 353 (1987); *Texas Lawyer*, 12 December 1994; *Austin American-Statesman*, 8 December 1994; United Press International, 29 September 1989.

David Powell is an exception to the rule that only the poor and those with little chance in the world

are sentenced to death. He is white, middle class, and smart.

Powell has been battling psychiatric problems for years. His family has a history of mental illness. Before his trouble with the law, Powell was medicating himself with street drugs. After spending time with him, you start to feel that he has consumed all the oxygen in the room. He's exhausting. A high-IQ student, he has the reputation of having made the highest score on the Texas college entrance exam.

Powell occupies his time in prison with mental exercises. He once devised his own random number generator by flipping a coin over and over. Then, using a mathematical formula, he composed a musical score.

So I sit down with my little hand calculator . . . and a pencil and paper and a dime . . . and I'm flipping this dime recording the outcomes, right . . . heads or tails. I don't know, five hundred, a thousand times or something to get a random input which I'm going to feed into this function. . . . It's going to spit out a rhythmic variation of this Mozart piece, right. . . .

So I flip and I flip and I flip and I write and then I start the number crunching and I compute and compute and I compute. By the time

I finish I've sworn I'll never do this again. . . . Had it figured, realized why, for years, I've put this off. . . . This is not work fit for human beings. It's too monotonous.

At length, I have a piece of music. And the piece of music I used and the scheme I used to compose it, as such, just as a flourish, you take the piece of music and if it were on one page which it wasn't . . . you can flip it upside down and play it. It would be the same piece. It had that type of symmetry.

We got a copy of the piece from one of his psychologists. He'd composed it without much experience in music. Those with exceptional intelligence must find life on death row to be especially excruciating.

Powell got caught up in drugs while in school. When he was arrested he had a cache of amphetamines. I'm sure he thought that with his intelligence he could control or beat their influence. But with his mental illness, he could not.

Of all the interviews we conducted, Powell's was the most unpredictable. Against his better judgment, he allowed us to meet with him. Expressing his displeasure with our "lack of preparation," he told me exactly what he thought of me and my entourage.

Powell was still thin as a fence post; nervous energy and prison food helped to keep him lean. In the all-white room, in the all-white uniform, his ghostly pallor blended into the background. While sitting he was all angles—elbows, jutting jaw, crisscrossed legs. Standing, he was a raw nerve. In my mind's eye I saw the photograph that I would eventually take before David even entered my frame. He lingered uncomfortably in my viewfinder for a couple of exposures, then told me he wanted to sit down. I didn't think we would finish the meeting with any civility.

As the session progressed, David's distrust subsided and he grew more engaging. I asked him questions with global and political implications, and he fielded them with intelligence and reflection. Then we broached the more personal subject of how the press treats death-row inmates.

In Texas, the media is so bad that I tend to think . . . maybe I haven't thought through the implications of this. This may be a very bad idea but it used to be, in Eastern Europe, one of the things they would do in reporting crime is instead of having sensationalistic slasher stories every day, they would have composite crime figures published every so often. I think that's probably a better way to approach the problem. If nothing else, it stands to reason that it would inspire less copycat crime. But it lends itself to more objective discussion too. More objective assimilation of the information.

David's ideas are usually well thought-out and worthy of consideration, even if they are somewhat odd.

On that day at Ellis I, sweat was dripping down my shirt collar. But though I was weighed down by the humidity, I did not want this unique man to slip away from me. I changed my tactics, moving constantly, cutting down angles, and blocking his escape. He parried beautifully.

Because of my conflicting emotions about Powell, this chapter was the most difficult for me to write. Describing his broken genius was harder than I imagined. But despite the wobbly start, I grew to appreciate David. Two years after we met he called and explained that he had not been at his best during our interview. He would have called sooner, but this was the first time he had had access to a phone: he had been transferred to a local jail where he was awaiting retrial. Released from the day-to-day strain of death row, David Powell has become a friend and a champion of our project.

You asked me what I feel about executions. I have no idea. Execution is very hard to accept. But, this place is the kind of environment that makes you not fear death.

The act of murder is an admission of one's inability to solve a dilemma in any other way. The state of Texas solves its problems with lethal injections.

Jim Vanderbilt

Nº 560

Ellis I Unit   Huntsville, Texas

Year of birth	1952
Marital status	divorced
Children	unknown
Date of offense	April 1, 1975
Sentenced to death	May 26, 1976
Status	pending resentencing

According to the Texas Court of Criminal Appeals, Jim Vanderbilt, a probationary police officer, abducted sixteen-year-old Katina Moyer at gunpoint from an Amarillo high school on April 1, 1975. He handcuffed her, took her to his house, and shot her in the back of the head. Vanderbilt, who had completed three years of college, had been fired a few days before the crime, for allegedly striking a traffic violator with a flashlight.

Source: *Vanderbilt v State*, 563 SW2d 590 (1978); *Austin American-Statesman*, 18 November 1995.

When I started this project I sought out Danny Lyons's seminal book, *Conversations with the Dead* (1971). After Texas I was startled to discover that Lyons, too, had taken photographs at the Texas Department of Corrections: I recognized the locations. Somehow, over twenty years later, I had retraced some of his steps. As we turned our van onto the dirt road leading to the Ellis I Unit, we were shocked to see the inmates performing the same ancient rituals Lyons had shot twenty years earlier. To my amazement, I was allowed to go out into the fields to photograph "the line": big men with tall hats, high up on horseback, overseeing dark prison work crews. Nothing seemed to move in the heat but the long rows of men manually chopping grass. It was an anachronism. Later, when I compared my photographs with Lyons's, I was surprised. Though his were in black and white, mine in color, the similarities were overwhelming. The inmates looked identical.

Death row is like the nuclear reactor core of a prison. When you enter you are slowly contaminated, in soul if not in body. No one leaves untainted. In this cauldron Jim Vanderbilt resides. Because he was once a cop, he has been ostracized by the prison community. This mild-mannered man is treated badly by everyone: the inmates hate him because he was one of the enemy; the security guards distrust him because he went bad.

And in here, there's no such thing as an ex-cop. You're a cop. . . . I cannot deal with the guards on a friendly basis. They cannot stand in front of my cell and talk to me. . . . But it causes me to have to be rude to people that in other circumstances I would be friendly with. . . .

Anytime someone snitches, I'm on the top of the list for—for possibilities. And because of it, one, I make it my business not to know someone else's business. So if I don't know then I couldn't . . . I'm eliminated. And if no one's standing in front of my cell, then I couldn't have said nothing to them. And I haven't talked to someone off the wing. They'll periodically take you down to the office and talk to you about this or that. And I haven't done that since '89. . . . Because everyone knows and no one forgets.

Talking to us meant that Jim was putting himself at risk. The unwritten rule on death row is to remain invisible: do your time without fanfare and live longer.

Jim Vanderbilt once petitioned for and won the right to grow his hair long. (He claimed his religion did not allow him to cut it.) For a time he was extremely hirsute; now he was clean-cut and scrubbed. His appearance is average: medium height, medium build. But for many on the Row, ordinary is a disguise, a cloak worn to make them appear no different from the rest of us. I once spent a lot of time photographing guerrilla warfare in Central America. The men I shot were stone-cold killers. I was convinced their character would always betray them; but they had no special aura.

Some inmates may even convince themselves that they haven't changed, when in fact they are forever changed. The decision to kill is a one-way street that reconfigures the psyche. And according to Vanderbilt, once on death row there's another transformation.

And one of the tragic things about the death penalty is that they almost never execute the man they convict or the man who committed the offense. Just assume the person's guilty. They . . . everyone changes in time. Well, death row escalates that change either for good or bad. It doesn't always—it's not always change for good. But it escalates it because you spend so much time alone. In my eighteen years I would dare say that I've spent at least fourteen years of that, second per second, by myself. And that changes you. . . .

And things like that are what, when I say, they don't kill the same person. It's not possible to express remorse in any way that can't be ridiculed.

I ate lunch at the commissary, surrounded by badges. Jim ate his meal while answering our questions (he had fish, "the best meal of the week"). While Jim wolfed down his meal, I shot pictures (I never said my intent was to flatter). It wasn't my idea of the ideal photo session, but I made the best of it.

Jim Vanderbilt is an aristocrat among inmates. Convicted of murder in the course of a kidnapping, he has survived well past the average life expectancy (just over nine years) on death row. In fact, he has been there over twenty years— longer than all but a handful of inmates in the

In a couple of years, it'll be half my life I've been locked up. And I'd never been arrested before. Just, I guess I start at the top. . . . Just barely twenty-two when I got arrested. And I was basically a student all my life. I got out of high school, right into college and, and I married about nine months before I got arrested. . . . Kind of feel like in a lot of ways I've never lived a life. The . . . my way of dealing with prison is to eliminate the "out there." That makes it easier to be "in here." It also makes it harder to establish and keep relationships like with Lisa [Radelet].

In the group of inmates we met in Texas, Jim does not stand out. He was loquacious and generous with his time, but he never meant to make a lasting connection. He did not try to conceal his lack of interest. His eyes conveyed no emotion, and he accepted none from us. In most of his conversations he failed to reveal himself, and he never revealed how he felt about his victim. He tended to confuse innocence with guilt.

I had someone say to me about a year and a half ago—they were complaining how hard it is to be on death row and be innocent. And I kind of got on to them and told them I'd trade with them in a hot second. Because they say to themselves when they see what appears to be the entire world saying, "You're a sorry animal, sucker." They can say, O.K., that they don't know. People who *are* guilty cannot help but say sometimes, "Are they right?"

It is interesting that the states and counties where lynching was most prevalent are today the ones that rely most heavily on the death penalty to solve their problems. The death penalty is not a solution to our violent culture; it is a symptom of it. Harris County, which encompasses the city of Houston, has been responsible for more executions in the United States in the last twenty years than any other entire state except Texas. Huntsville's seven prisons are its principal industry. So it made some kind of sense that the most populous death row in the country was also the most fruitful for us.

When it comes down to it, Vanderbilt didn't owe me anything. We weren't there to become friends; we were there to take his picture. We have never heard from him since.

PAMELA LYNN PERILLO

Nº 665

Mountain View Unit   Gatesville, Texas

Year of birth   1955
Marital status   single
Children   one
Date of offense   February 23, 1980
Sentenced to death   September 2, 1980
Status   under appeal

In March 1980, Pamela Lynn Perillo hailed a police officer in Denver, Colorado. Later, at police headquarters, she gave a full confession. She, James Michael Briddle, and Briddle's wife, Pamela Fletcher, had hitchhiked from California to Texas to avoid apprehension for an armed robbery. On February 21, 1980, they had been picked up in Houston by Bob Banks. Banks was in the process of moving, and had agreed to let the three stay at his house in exchange for their help. A friend of his, Bob Skeens, would also help.

On February 23, the three hitchhikers decided to rob Banks and Skeens. They bound the two men and strangled them with a nylon rope. After taking various items from the house, they fled in Skeens's car.

Tried separately in 1980, Briddle and Perillo were sentenced to death. In both trials the state's

chief witness was Pamela Fletcher, who claimed she had not participated in the killings. She was subsequently sentenced to five years of probation. An error in jury selection won Perillo a second trial, but in November 1980 she was reconvicted and was again sentenced to death.

Source: *Perillo v State*, 758 SW2d 567 (Tex Cr App 1988); *Perillo v State*, 656 SW2d 78 (Tex Cr App 1983).

This project was never intended to be academic; I'm more interested in metaphors than statistics. Because my sample of death-row inmates was very small, I had to be careful not to leap to conclusions that logic would not support. But one striking theme kept surfacing in case after case: child abuse. Being abused as a child, or witnessing domestic battering, is the environmental factor most often cited as a contributor to juvenile violence. It is a large part of a complicated formula swelling the American prison population.

Fifteen years ago, Pam Perillo left California to escape arrest and a life of drugs, crime, and abuse. Headed for Florida in search of a new life, she stopped in Texas for what she thought would be two days.

My mother died when I was ten and when she died, my father started drinking a lot and became an alcoholic and there was sexual abuse between my sister and myself with him and my sister was taken away to live with relatives from Iowa. And I was running away from home and then I was put in foster homes. I was in eight different foster homes and I was made a ward of the court and taken from my father's custody. I started using drugs when I was eleven and just lived a very crazy life after that and my father was arrested for sexual abuse. I turned him in. I turned him in to a friend. She told her mom and they told the police and all that and he had to go and take the lie detector test. . . . I was twelve.

In 1980, Pam became the first woman to be sentenced to death in Texas since 1963. The media's portrayal of her case was so distorted, she has refused all interviews since then. Geraldo Rivera and Montel Williams are among the many who have unsuccessfully requested interviews with her. One of fewer than fifty women on death row in the United States—six of them in Texas—Pam chooses to maintain a low profile. But it's hard for her to remain anonymous.

Every time they write an article about death row and about women on death row or every time my fall partner [James Briddle] does something stupid over there, my name is dragged right through it. . . . My fall partner is involved in the Aryan Brotherhood, which is the white-racist thing and he's tried to kill several black men over there and every time he does something stupid, my name is right there in the paper. Two days before I was going to trial the second time, he made a homemade bomb . . . and threw it in and burnt this guy really bad, really bad, and it was all in the paper about him doing it and his involvement in the Aryan Brotherhood and there my name was. . . .

Although she admits the prison routine is not as bad as it could be, time has not been good to Pam. She chain smokes; when she turns the wrong way, she appears almost feral. She has more tattoos than she cares to count. On the day we were visiting, she wore makeup: eyeliner, eye shadow, mascara, lipstick, and very red fingernails.

Pam dealt carefully with all the questions we asked her. As emotional as she sometimes seemed, she never appeared to break. It was impossible to know whether it was the years in prison that had taught her to keep herself in such complete control. She convinced us she was not afraid to die. Though in jail excuses are legion, she never blamed anyone or anything for her fate.

You know, it's strange but when I was out there using heroin all the time, I used to say, "I'm a hope-to-die dope fiend and when I die I'm going to die with a needle in my arm." And never did I even imagine I would end up in Texas where they kill you by lethal injection.

Though she never married, Pam is a mother. Her son and his adopted grandmother visit once a month, driving three hours each way. He has never known her outside of jail. When he started asking questions about why other prisoners were getting out, but she wasn't, she told him the truth.

Yeah, he understood. He fell apart when I told him that I could be executed. He took it really hard. . . . We both cried and it was very hard because I wanted to hug him and I couldn't [there are no contact visits in Texas]. . . . We just all sat there for four hours crying and talking and being honest. He's not ashamed of where I am. . . . He'll tell anybody his mother's in prison.

I belatedly realized I was talking to a woman accused of killing another human being. Murder seems such a masculine act. In fact, 90 percent of violent criminals are men.

Our victims [the people we kill] aren't the only victims. Our families are the victims and our children are the victims. They go through this too. So that, you know, we have not only hurt our victims' families but we—we're hurting our own. . . .

The ever-present female prison guard nodded that our time was up. We said our goodbyes. Pam, like every prisoner, was strip-searched after leaving us. I found her unused hand-rolled cigarettes discarded in a trash can: time and effort wasted.

With sixteen years on death row, Pam's chances of receiving a reprieve are dwindling. She was once awarded a new trial, but the jury reconvicted her and sentenced her to death. Soon after we visited Pam, her new execution date was announced. Jim Briddle was executed in the winter of 1995. On Mother's Day in 1995 Pam received another stay of her execution.

James H. Roane, Jr.

Nº 206197

Powhatan Correctional Center
State Farm, Virginia

Year of birth	1965
Marital status	married
Children	five
Date of offense	January–February 1992
Sentenced to death	February 16, 1993
Status	under appeal

Indicted under a 1989 federal statute, James H. Roane, Jr., Cory Johnson, and Richard Tipton were accused of eleven drug-related murders committed in Richmond, Virginia, in 1992. The state argued that the three men had been importing cocaine from New York to Richmond, where they used it to manufacture crack. Their victims included people who owed them money as well as innocent bystanders.

The three men were tried together in 1993. Johnson was convicted of seven murders, Tipton of six, and Roane of three. Johnson received seven death sentences; Tipton, three; Roane, one death sentence and two life.

Source: *Legal Intelligencer*, 17 February 1993; *Washington Post*, 17 February 1993, 29 April 1992.

The United States, with its long history of revolution, frontiersmanship, and imperialism, has spawned a people that solve their problems with a big stick. The cowboys of yesteryear are the gang members of today. Three members of the Newton Gang, an inner-city, drug-trafficking ring, are housed today at Powhatan Correctional Center. They are together doing their time and awaiting their fate. We met one, Federal Prison No. 206197. His story is centered in Richmond, whose crime-plagued ghetto produces many victims.

The RICO Act and the Crime Bills of 1988 and 1994 were supposed to combat white collar crime as well as the less sophisticated but equally well

organized inner city gangs. Racketeering is the reason we came to know James H. Roane, Jr.

On our way to the guards' offices, we had brushed past a tall, well-built Black man dressed in prison orange and shackled hand and foot. Later, when he shuffled in with three guards, we were embarrassed to discover that he was our subject. We apologized. But our callousness did not faze Roane a bit. He was starving to be heard. He didn't need our sympathy. He needed our attention.

And I left home to get with a girl. And I'd go back to that neighborhood and I was starting to use drugs. I started using drugs at the age of maybe thirteen. And I did every . . . I've experienced smoking crack, IV drug user. You name it. And it developed into a habit. And I turned to drugs to make me happy. I . . . felt like somebody. . . . It made me feel like I accomplished something, that I could do anything. And so I had a lot of experiences with drugs.

Roane had been on death row only a few months, so his energy level was still high. He spoke in an accelerated staccato in a visiting room so cramped we didn't have room to move. He talked of growing up in the inner city.

Because, as a kid, in the violence and destruction that I grew up in, it was a crime-infested neighborhood. . . . You always had to fight. And I never really liked fighting. But, if you went to the store, you knew you had to fight. If

you was on the school bus, you had to fight. . . . You've got to be tough. You've got to fight.

The pressure of growing up too fast had had a bad effect on him. So many citizens are caught in the purgatory between violence and drugs. The claustrophobia causes them to make the kinds of mistakes that James Roane made.

And I had like five kids and I wasn't a father. I would go see them and I wanted to do for them, but I didn't know how to. Because I didn't have no experience in working. I didn't have no education and I didn't have no skills. So it made it much more difficult for me. And I really had nobody to really talk to because I didn't talk to people. . . . I didn't care about living. . . . All I wanted to do was live to get high.

In trouble since he was nine, James regretted the direction he had taken. He tried to get help. He pleaded with a judge, enrolled in programs designed to assist substance abusers. But eventually he fell back into his old habits.

Well, you know, it felt like everything was failing that I tried to do right. And so I started selling drugs. And in the drug life, it's an addiction. Dealing is an addiction. . . . It become habit forming.

Often people who turn to gangs are so disenfranchised they see crime as a reasonable means of "taking care of business." Drug dealing offers fast, easy money to young people for whom opportunities are minimal. Dealing drugs brought Roane a certain degree of respect in the depressed neighborhood. It was like helping an extended family.

And they would come to me and they would say, "Junior, you know, you want me to go to the store for you?" And to me, I know what that means, "I think that I'm hungry. My mom is probably somewhere smoking crack and I don't know how to ask. . . ." So that was a form of crying out and saying, "I'm hungry." And even though I wasn't hungry at the time, because I had a little money, I would say, "Well, just pick me up a soda, you know, get you and your sister something to eat." And so one of those little guys I called and said, "Dig." And they'd say, "We're doing in school . . . football . . . I've got a job at the corner store now. . . ." And that's the gratitude I get for helping.

No federal death-row inmate has been executed since 1963. Federal laws are seen as filling gaps in state regulations; people demand new laws to ensnare more criminals and punish them more severely. More violators are imprisoned with heavier sentences, and the courts are struggling to keep up the pace.

Because this is a federal death row, it is a bigger, more convoluted maze. The statutes are complicated; the red tape is endless. We were able to get in only because of having been on other death rows—we were veterans. We were nevertheless a royal pain as far as the administration was concerned. We had to dicker for every concession. There was not enough room to set up for the shoot; we insisted on leaving some doors open so we could spread out. We were thus in full view of everyone moving in and out of the area.

While all around looked on, Roane, crammed into a six-by-nine-foot cubicle, related poignant details of his friendships, specifically one with a friend who had committed suicide.

But anyway, he would always talk to me, as we got older, about change. And I never paid him no mind, you know, because I was always high and I always wanted to live life on my terms and not on life's terms. So while I was locked up, he really—preparing for trial, he killed himself. . . . At that point, I felt like I didn't have the desire to live. . . . Because it was always me and him. We always struggled. . . . We laughed together. We cried together. We were hungry together. . . . It just changed my life. Because I learned about things that I already had in me that I didn't even know that I had to know. And I always looked to get it from other people. And now I don't today. I get it from me.

In the middle of the interview, Roane suddenly commented that all his life he'd liked having his picture taken. He had wanted once to be a model. I think he envisioned this as the closest thing possible to a *GQ* photo spread.

Jack Foster Outten, Jr.

Nº 180640

Multi-Purpose Criminal Justice Facility
Wilmington, Delaware

Year of birth	1966
Marital status	single
Children	one
Date of offense	January 12, 1992
Sentenced to death	April 30, 1993
Status	under appeal

On January 11, 1992, Jack Foster Outten, Jr., spent the afternoon drinking beer with two cousins, Nelson and Steven Shelton, and Nelson's girlfriend, Christina Gibbons. That evening, at a bar in New Castle, Delaware, they met sixty-four-year-old Wilson Mannon. The group left the bar with Mannon, whose body was found the next day, beaten to death with the top of a washing machine. At trial the state's principal witness was Gibbons, who claimed at first that Steven was uninvolved in the murder. All three men were sentenced to death.

Source: *Outten and Shelton v State*, 650 A2d 1,291 (1994); *New York Times*, 18 March 1995.

It isn't etiquette to cut anyone you've been introduced to. Remove the joint!

—Lewis Carroll

The guard pointed to a doorway almost fifty feet away, at the far end of the control module. It was so dark I could barely make out the room. Taking initiative in this environment can be dangerous. In the confusion I walked closer to the open door and whispered, "Jack? Jack Outten?" Suddenly a hand thrust out of the darkness to meet mine.

Introductions are always awkward in prison. No one exchanges pleasantries—those who rarely get to go outdoors do not chat about the weather. We mumbled back and forth for a few minutes; I motioned Lorie over to help relieve the tension. I still could not see his face. A guard spirited me away, wanting to talk about the logistics of our photographs. He seemed unconcerned that he was leaving a male prisoner with a young woman. I did not take my eyes off the door to that room.

*What other dungeon is so dark as one's own
heart! What jailer so inexorable as one's self!*
                                          —Nathaniel Hawthorne

The Multi-Purpose Criminal Justice Facility
(MPCJF) had had a power failure just before we
arrived. The jailers had not known what to do
with us. We were worried we would be denied
entry. It was visiting day, and they had had to
turn away friends and relatives—people who had
traveled a long way to see their loved ones.

You will find it shall echo my speech to a T.
                                          —Thomas Moore

They moved us from one room to another. The
light was blindingly bright. The entire ceiling was
covered with green-white fluorescent tubes, accompanied by a 120-cycle hum. The concrete-
block walls reflected sound so efficiently that the
echo rendered three hours' worth of our audio
tapes unusable.

In the light, Jack Outten at first looked like a
tough guy. Tattoos covered his hands and arms.
One in particular stood out—SWP; it proclaimed
his membership in the racist organization Supreme White Power.

At the MPCJF, death-row inmates live among the
general prison population. They have the same
privileges and the same restrictions. The facility
is crowded well beyond the capacity for which it
was designed, 720 prisoners. (At the time of our

visit it held over eleven hundred). Jack shares his cell with multiple roommates, with whom he must play musical beds. Some prisoners are forced to sleep in waiting and interview rooms.

Although Jack had been convicted with two cousins, they were kept in different prisons. I later photographed one of his cousins, Nelson Shelton, but neither mentioned the other during the interviews. It became clear they did not get along anymore. With the death penalty, sooner or later everybody loses.

Outten rambled on about his past. His father had been hard on him. Before his arrest, Jack had been a carpenter, working seven days a week. He'd fathered two children, one of whom had died in infancy. Their mother visited him nearly every week. He had had some previous run-ins with the law—he claimed to be a thief by nature—and had spent two years in jail for various offenses. He hadn't given the death penalty a thought in those days.

Goddammit, look! We live here and they live there. We black and they white. They got things and we ain't. They do things and we can't. It's just like living in jail.
— Richard Wright

Jack said he knew exactly what had happened the night of the murder, but would not say. We prodded him gently, but he would tell us no more than what he had said in court.

There I was, a Black photographer talking intimately with a white murderer who swore allegiance to a white-supremacist group. If we had met at a party, we might not have talked to each other. Here we tried to be friends.

A state is not a mere society, having a common place, established for the prevention of mutual crime and for the sake of exchange. . . . Political society exists for the sake of noble actions, and not of mere companionship.
— Aristotle

The death penalty is a very emotional issue, and debates are usually decided before they begin. Arguments contain little new information and minds are rarely changed. Capital crimes, though, represent only a tiny fraction of all crimes committed in this country. We spend so much time, money, and energy on that small number of crimes that we have little left with which to address the remainder of our huge crime problem, to initiate programs that might actually be effective.

This is not to downplay the needs of homicide victims' friends and families, who deserve our help and sympathy. Their anger, even their desire for retribution, is understandable. But as a society, we need to maintain our objectivity, and we must not be diverted from the battle to prevent similar crimes. And we must be above the violence, the need for revenge, seeking rather to understand and confront our problems, not accepting social Band-Aids or trying to get even.

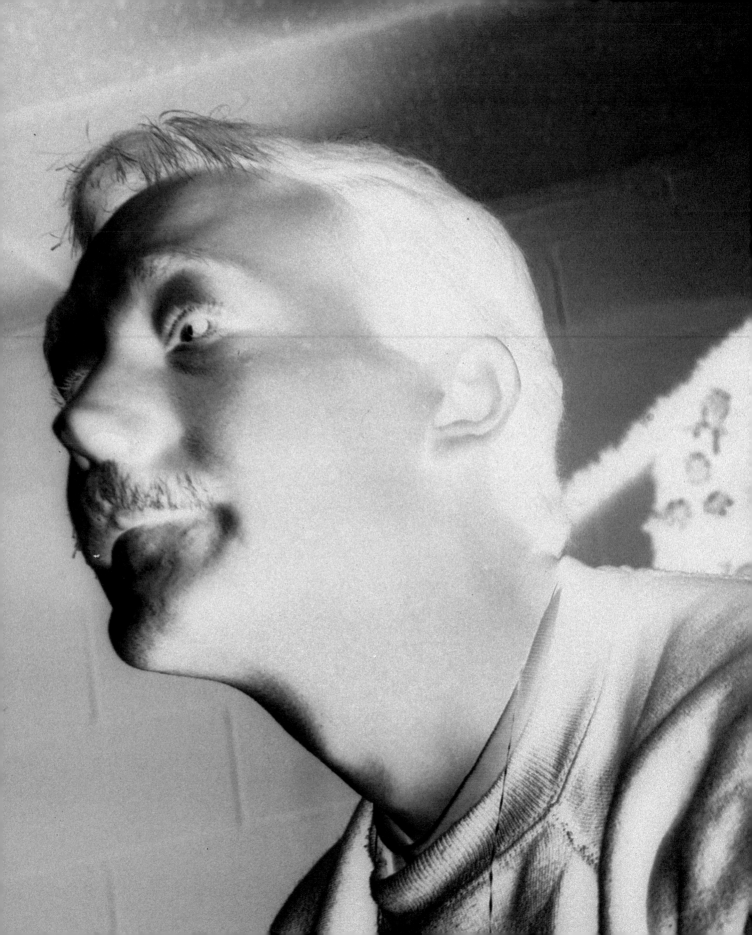

NELSON SHELTON

Nº 165919

Sussex Correctional Institution
Georgetown, Delaware

Year of birth	1968
Marital status	single
Children	one
Date of offense	January 12, 1992
Sentenced to death	April 30, 1993
Status	executed March 17, 1995, by lethal injection

On January 11, 1992, Nelson Shelton spent the afternoon drinking beer with his brother Steven, his cousin Jack Outten, and his girlfriend, Christina Gibbons. That evening, at a bar in New Castle, Delaware, they met sixty-four-year-old Wilson Mannon. The group left the bar with Mannon, whose body was found the next day, beaten to death with the top of a washing machine. At trial the state's principal witness was Gibbons, who claimed at first that Nelson's brother was uninvolved in the murder. All three men were sentenced to death. Nelson decided not to appeal and was executed in 1995.

Source: *Outten and Shelton v State*, 650 A2d 1,291 (1994); *New York Times*, 18 March 1995.

Nelson Shelton could not have been more different from his cousin Jack Outten. He entered the interview room crestfallen. A death-penalty "volunteer," he had ordered his lawyer not to appeal his sentence. Many see this as state-assisted suicide. His rationale was that if he could not work, he might as well die.

What I miss most? The morning part. I had a lot of problems, but I loved to work. And I guess it comes from my father. . . . I was always the first one on the job site. And I was just going along with the mornings.

During his time on death row, he stared back at a life that didn't seem worth continuing. He didn't like what he saw; his conscience was acting

up. Like so many others, he sought salvation in religion.

Having found God, Nelson was reduced to meekness. He moved very little; his words came painfully. It was hard to tell whether he was speaking from the heart or just parroting phrases from his new-found religion. He seemed sincerely resigned to his death.

Well, yeah, the death penalty is O.K. and it's suitable. And I'm pretty much comfortable with that because I believe in the Holy Bible and I believe in every wonder that's in there. . . . And it was right after the flood, when God told Moses, his son would be proof and multiply. . . . And God set a few guidelines, a few laws down. And one of the first laws was if any man shall shed any man's blood, by man shall that man's blood be shed. And that was right.

To support his reasoning and prove his point, Nelson relied on Scripture. His conclusions may have been questionable, but he backed them with his life.

Nelson's life of crime came back to torture both his sleeping and waking hours. Influenced by his older brother, who had taught him to be aggressive, Nelson had gotten deeper and deeper into trouble. Now he was taking medication to keep the memories from overpowering him.

Recently, I tried some antidepressant medication. I wouldn't let them put me on those Thorazine or Halcion or any of that stuff. And I'm on just a regular, generic antidepressant, because I was sleeping too much. I was putting in sixteen, twelve hours in bed. And sleeping through meals and everything. . . . I've been going, trying to struggle with a normal routine for the last week. It helps with the medication, the antidepressant.

Nelson had had little success in school, where he alternated between the roles of class clown and class bully. His few good moments were eclipsed by repeated stints in juvenile detention. Called slow all his life, he had to search for the words to put his education into perspective.

My dad used to always call me stupid. Literally. And I didn't know anything. Because no one showed me nothing. Not one person showed me anything that was right. Not one.

While I was photographing Nelson there were long periods of silence. The room was deafeningly quiet, with only the hum of a distant fan or air conditioner to break the hush. I felt like a voyeur. Nervous, I hung on his excruciatingly labored responses. He was near tears.

I thought about the effect I was having on Nelson. Every photographer must address the fact that all photography is exploitation. On death row, my presence is a transgression at any time, but in Nelson Shelton's case, it was obvious from the

first. By interviewing him I exacerbated his problems, forced him to confront his guilt even more.

And now I think about that man [Wilson Mannon]. And I think about his family and what his family's going through. . . . Even though my father was rough with me and had a bad fuse, you know, to brutally kill like that—. . . . I know he was a real kind, gentle guy, you know. . . . And it's like he was getting ready to retire and enjoy life. And the way I see it now, is that before he could retire and enjoy the

fruits of his labor, you know, four evil people came along and snuffed his life out. And it wasn't right at all. No, I . . . I'm really torn. Even though my life is in the balance, you know.

Nelson Shelton was executed on March 17, 1995. His death created so little stir, I didn't hear about it until a month later.

NICHOLAS YARRIS

AM-6841

State Correctional Institution at Huntingdon
Huntingdon, Pennsylvania

Year of birth	1961
Marital status	married while on death row
Children	none
Date of offense	December 15, 1981
Sentenced to death	January 23, 1983
Status	under appeal

Nicholas Yarris was convicted of the rape and murder of thirty-three-year-old Linda Craig, whom he kidnapped at a shopping mall just before Christmas 1981. When Mrs. Craig failed to arrive home on time, her husband and a police officer began to search for her. They found her car parked along a desolate roadway. Early the next morning, her badly beaten body was found in a church parking lot. She had been stabbed six times.

Source: *Commonwealth v Yarris*, 549 A2d 513 (1988); United Press International, 18 October 1988, 14 March 1985, 24 January 1983.

Nicholas Yarris escaped after two years on death row. His hands hurt from being scraped in the fall down the hill, and he was bleeding. By instinct he eluded the helicopter and the dogs. It was February and it was cold. He ended up in Florida,

basking on sunny beaches, amazed at his new-found freedom. But after a month of running and hiding, he was arrested while sitting in a stolen car with a gun on the seat next to him. He freely admitted his identity and was soon on his way back to death row.

We corresponded with Yarris for nearly two years before we were granted permission to see him. Time after time the corrections department in Pennsylvania refused our requests. The NAACP Legal Defense Fund volunteered their resources, but their efforts were to no avail. Nick occasionally called us collect and we continued to write. Then we got lucky. Our nemesis, the assistant warden, was transferred. When permission finally was given, it was with the stipulation that Nick would be behind glass. Lorie Savel was able to convince another state's corrections department to intervene on our behalf. Her strategy eventually worked.

We flew to Pittsburgh during one of the biggest storms of a terrible winter. Our flight to Altoona was canceled, so we drove to Huntingdon in zero visibility on treacherous roads through one of the highest mountain passes in the state. The three-hour drive turned into five. We knew our visitation would be impossible to reschedule; we somehow arrived on time.

All his life Nicholas Yarris has exhibited a criminal mind. In his youth he had some success in sports, and even received a college athletic schol-

arship to play baseball. But before he could accept, he was arrested for burglary. It was not an isolated infraction.

In prison, Nick reads; he devours books. He has discovered all he missed when he wasn't able to accept that scholarship.

One of the best things that's ever happened to me was being locked down twenty-two hours a day. Because I had to not only deal with the demons that I dealt with as a child but I had to learn to educate myself and develop myself.

Yarris is one of those inmates who got married on death row. His wedding is what originally piqued

our interest. We even asked permission to do a portrait of the bride and groom. But Nick has had only one contact visit with his wife, the day they were wed.

I wanted to take the absolute worst date of my life and change it. And that was July 1, 1982 [the date of his murder conviction]. I wanted to take that day and reverse it with something that really meant something to me. So we got married on July 1, 1988. . . . Boy, my folks were like. . . . It was really harmful to me because they didn't show up. They were going to. . . . I guess they couldn't handle it.

Nick's wife, Jacque, visits him religiously. She works tirelessly on his case. He and Jacque are continually trying to force the state of Pennsylvania to reexamine the evidence. He claims that DNA testing will prove his innocence. But in 1988 the chief justice of the Pennsylvania Supreme Court affirmed the jury's verdict. Still, they persist.

We thought we had gotten to know Yarris by reading his letters and talking with him long-distance. We were unprepared when we finally met him in person: we realized that he was not the same man. Laughing and animated over the phone, he was reserved face to face, introverted and insecure. The wisecracking banter we'd become used to showed itself only briefly. We tried to draw him out, to meld the two personas.

If someone sat in prison as I have, locked in a cell all day, focused on everything that they endure as a human being, I'm quite sure at some point they would become overwhelmed. So the rationale behind that is to try your best to make everything as pseudonormal as possible. In other words, I have to make it that my day begins a normal day. It's *not* a normal atmosphere.

Yarris paused between each syllable, to add emphasis.

Nick continues to call us collect to give us updates on his case. We try to pretend it is all normal.

MUMIA ABU-JAMAL

AM-8335

State Correctional Institution at Huntingdon
Huntingdon, Pennsylvania

Year of birth	1954
Marital status	married
Children	eight children, three grandchildren
Date of offense	December 9, 1981
Sentenced to death	July 2, 1982
Status	under appeal

At 3:55 A.M. on December 9, 1981, a Philadelphia police officer stopped a Volkswagen Beetle that had been traveling the wrong way down a one-way street. The car was driven by Mumia Abu-Jamal's brother, William Cook. Jamal, who was driving a taxi-cab nearby, stopped his vehicle and approached the scene. Minutes later, the police officer, Daniel Faulkner, lay dying of four bullet wounds.

Jamal's pistol was found at the scene. At trial, eyewitnesses pointed the finger at him. Forensic experts testified that the bullets that killed Faulkner could have been fired from Jamal's gun. But later investigation challenged their conclusion, and the testimony of the eyewitnesses was called into question when several new witnesses claimed

they had seen an unidentified man fleeing the scene.

Source: *Commonwealth v Abu-Jamal*, 555 A2d 846 (1989); *New York Times*, 13 August 1995, 14 July 1995; Mumia Abu-Jamal, *Live from Death Row* (Reading, Mass.: Addison-Wesley, 1995).

Early one morning in 1981, a Black man driving a taxi through the red-light district of Philadelphia encountered an altercation. On closer investigation, he saw it was a white policeman throttling a black youth—an all-too-familiar occurrence in the inner city. With a background as a social activist, Mumia Abu-Jamal couldn't avoid getting involved. Out of the car and into the fray, he recognized the person who was being beaten as his brother. What happened next is unclear, but when the fight was over the policeman lay dead, and Jamal had been severely injured. The truth about what happened depends on who is telling the story.

Born Wesley Cook, Mumia Abu-Jamal was raised in Philadelphia and graduated from Benjamin Franklin High School. He cofounded the Philadelphia branch of the Black Panther Party and served as its minister of information. A respected newspaperman, he later became the president of the Philadelphia Association of Black Journalists. To supplement his income, he moonlighted as a cab driver.

Many organizations and publications call Mumia a political prisoner.

First of all, let me begin with the proposition . . . my firm belief that every African American prisoner in American prisons is a political prisoner. By that I mean that it is a policy decision at the highest levels and the lowest levels of this system to incriminate, to incarcerate, to harass Black life through this system.

Mumia adheres to the teachings of John Africa, who founded the controversial MOVE sect based in Philadelphia. His Black-militant stance is evident in his actions, his oratory, and his writings. And was surely a factor in his sentencing.

Jamal's religion is manifested in his long dreadlocks. His assertion that cutting his hair would violate his religious beliefs continues to confound the Department of Corrections, which had placed him in disciplinary confinement. His hairstyle, his lifestyle, his political and personal beliefs—all have contributed to his imprisonment and the harassment he continues to be subject to.

I remember one very respected newspaper in Philadelphia described MOVE as the lowest form of human species. It is not odd or out of the ordinary, to hear, to read, in whatever medium in Philadelphia, MOVE described, not just demonized but animalized, dehumanized. That's the norm.

Mumia took his time with us. His attentiveness and commitment paralleled ours. He was very honest and uncompromising about his situation, but it was very hard to distinguish the rhetoric from what was sincere.

A known agitator, Mumia was a firebrand in the Philadelphia press, constantly antagonizing the political powers. He disliked the police; the police returned the sentiment. His editorials appeared during one of the city's darkest political periods. Jamal saw a connection between his journalism and my project on death row.

So that you know when we talk about doing this project [photographs of death-row inmates] in a way that humanizes people who are the most condemned in American society, that is an extension of the work I did as a reporter: to try to humanize people that I knew on a human level as extraordinary, beautiful human beings.

When he was arrested, tried, and convicted, the press that had once at least tolerated him turned on him.

At the time of our interview, Jamal had spent over fifteen years fighting his conviction. His appeals are based on the charge that Philadelphia courts are racist. Nationwide, only in Los Angeles and Harris County, Texas, have more people been sentenced to death. Only 9 percent of Pennsylvania's population, African Americans account for over 60 percent of those on death row. The Philadelphia District Attorney's Office sought the death penalty in 50 percent of all homicide cases at the time of Mumia's conviction.

Failing to get relief in the courts, Jamal and his supporters have launched a grassroots campaign that has captured national and international attention. It was a big gamble on his part, certain to aggravate the authorities. Jamal probably has more media visibility than anyone else on death row in the United States. From his cell he has written for the *Yale Law Journal* and the *Philadelphia Inquirer*. His comments have been broadcast on over a hundred radio stations around the nation. Recently Jamal published a collection of essays, *Live from Death Row*, which has evoked a storm of controversy over convicts' rights. An inquiry is currently under way to determine whether he can legally enter into a contract or conduct business as a ward of the state.

Jamal's face now appears in bookstore windows, on graffiti-covered walls, and in mimeographed fliers all over the world. Many serious observers believe in his innocence, or at least that justice has not been served. Celebrities have rallied to his cause, among them E. L. Doctorow, Norman Mailer, Oliver Stone, Alice Walker, Paul Newman, Sting, Roger Ebert, Susan Sarandon, and Maya Angelou. Every serious talk show has covered his case, and the rapper KRS-One has recorded a song called "Free Mumia."

For Jamal, our project was a rare opportunity for personal contact. It sparked some inner turmoil.

This is the first time I've met another human being other than a guard since July of 1983 without handcuffs or shackles. . . . I don't know what my children, my wife, my brother, I don't know what they feel like anymore. Because, were we to meet . . . it would be a Plexiglas shield down here and a little steel-mesh, wire-mesh area down here where sound can travel through but where no touching is permitted.

Frankly, I'm a little uncomfortable. I've been shackled for so long I feel uncomfortable right now . . . in the sense that the prison administrators agreed to allow us to do this project but would forbid me to hug my wife, or my children, or my grandchildren at this stage.

He complained that when we left he would be disrobed and submitted to a full body cavity search. (Even after visitations in shackles and behind glass, he had to do the same.)

Since our meeting with Jamal, the Pennsylvania Department of Corrections has been holding him incommunicado—no visits from anyone except his family and lawyers. Unable to interview him, news services have approached us for photographs. Pleas for help from his supporters have increased exponentially.

All this began with a traffic ticket on a one-way street.

Michael B. Ross

Nº 127404

Somers Correctional Institution
Somers, Connecticut

Year of birth	1959
Marital status	single
Children	none
Date of offenses	1982–1984
Sentenced to death	July 6, 1987
Status	pending resentencing

Michael B. Ross was convicted of the kidnapping, rape, and murder of four teenage girls in New London, Connecticut, in 1983 and 1984, as well as the murder of two other young women in 1982. A 1981 graduate of Cornell University, Ross was an insurance salesman in the Norwich area. On his arrest in June 1984, he confessed to strangling the women and raping all but one.

At trial, Ross's defense attorneys did not contest his guilt; instead, Ross pleaded insanity. He failed to convince the jury. At his sentencing, his attorneys argued that he suffered from extreme emotional disturbance and an abusive childhood—factors they contended should spare him from the electric chair. Ross was the first person to be sentenced to death under a statute enacted by the Connecticut state legislature seven years earlier.

In 1994 Ross wrote to several newspapers to announce that he was dropping his appeals and requesting execution. Then, because the trial court had excluded evidence that would have supported a life sentence, he won a new hearing from the Connecticut Supreme Court. At the end of 1995, Ross was trying to fire his attorneys and waive the new hearing.

Source: *State v Ross*, 646 A2d 1,318 (1994); *New York Times*, 17 February 1994, 7 July 1987, 27 June 1987, 14 December 1985.

Very first feeling I had was my heart pounding. It was really pounding and then the next feeling was my hands hurt because I manually strangled them and my fingers were all cramped and then the third feeling I remember was fear coming in, "Oh, my God, there's a dead body in front of me," and that's when I would hide the bodies and go through all that.

Michael Ross doesn't remember actually strangling the women he killed. But we were being entrusted with the deep, dark memories of this condemned man. Michael was a predator. His victims, ranging in age from fourteen to twenty-six, were faceless to him.

I would think anyway that I should have in my mind a picture of what they looked like when I was strangling them, when I was killing them, and I don't. I have no idea of what they looked like. My only recollection of what they looked like was what was in the newspapers afterwards, like the high school picture or whatever.

At college and after, Ross raped and murdered while at the same time maintaining normal relationships with girlfriends.

They were saying that when I'm with one type of women, when I'm with one that pampers me, takes care of me, loving type of woman, I don't hurt anybody. When I'm in an aggressive relationship with someone who fights and we bicker and we argue all the time, then that's

when I go out and hurt people. . . . With one relationship, I killed four people. Then I was in
another relationship where I didn't kill anybody. Then I was in another relationship where
I killed four people and they call it something
like "splitting."

As he recounted his sins, sun streamed into the
dark, silent space from huge windows. Michael
sat bathed in sunlight, his khaki uniform starched
and pressed. His account was delivered so mat-
ter-of-factly. These were real lives he was talking
about, yet to him they were anonymous. It's the

serial killers, with their insatiable urges, who capture the public's attention. Michael Ross was a serial murderer, so his crimes had produced large headlines. I had sought Ross out because I needed to include a worst case in my project. It's so easy for the public to cry for execution, but I wanted to illuminate the sympathetic and the heinous with the same light.

Michael attributes his problems to mental imbalance: he could not control his emotions. Troubled in childhood by his fantasies, he became more and more tormented in college.

But I guess the easiest way to explain it is everybody's had a tune that's been playing in their head, like a melody that they heard on the radio or something. It just plays over and over and over again. . . . I have that and no matter how hard you try to get rid of that melody, it's still there. And that could kind of drive you nuts. But if you replace that melody now with thoughts of rape and murder and degradation of women . . .

Sam Reese Sheppard, the son of the doctor who inspired the TV series and the movie *The Fugitive*, introduced us to Michael Ross. I had thought I would encounter a madman, a captive of Thorazine and the straitjacket. But because of modern pharmaceuticals, his life had changed. He did not fit my preconception of the archetypal serial killer. Ten years after his crimes, Ross was friendly, affable, even ebullient—he bounced. His hands moved in unison with his mouth; his curiosity and enthusiasm overwhelmed and slightly unsettled us. He had once been a handsome Ivy Leaguer, an engineering major. Somehow he had metamorphosed into a killer.

During his years on death row, Michael demonstrated his instability by appealing at different times to be executed, castrated, or retried. He even wrote an article for the *Hartford Courant*'s Sunday magazine titled "It's Time for Me to Die." Now, on therapeutic medications, Ross says he no longer has the fantasies that made him dangerous. They have been replaced by recurring dreams of his execution. No matter what scientists find out about him and his obsessions, mental illness or insanity, he will never be released. Death row is incurable.

If I'm executed or if I die, I just want to be cremated and my ashes scattered. I want no gravestone, no reminders, the name "Mike Ross: He's the guy who killed all those women." I just want to be forgotten.

TERRY JOHNSON

Nᴼ 183495

Somers Correctional Institution
Somers, Connecticut

Year of birth	1969
Marital status	single
Children	two
Date of offense	June 5, 1991
Sentenced to death	June 10, 1992
Status	under appeal

Terry Johnson was sentenced to death for the murder of Connecticut State Trooper Russell Bagshaw. He and his brother Duane were burglarizing a gun shop when Bagshaw arrived at the scene. Before Bagshaw could get out of his cruiser, Terry Johnson fired a semiautomatic pistol into the darkness. One of his bullets found a gap in Bagshaw's bulletproof vest. Terry Johnson pleaded guilty to the murder. His brother Duane received life in prison without parole.

Source: *New York Times*, 27 May 1993, 11 December 1992, 9 June 1991.

The sons of a former police officer, Terry and Duane Johnson were vilified by the press as cop killers. Duane was tried as an accomplice; he was eighteen at the time and barely involved in the crime—his older brother had dragged him along. Terry Johnson is now marking time on death row.

But being inside the prison walls is no protection from the condemnation he received on the outside. Now the corrections officers taunt him for killing one of their own.

You try to keep as low profile as you can to keep from getting flak. You know you'll be walking down the hall . . . "You're getting the electric chair, Joe." They'll make buzzing noises or "You're going to fry." Or they'll say,

"Can I get a side order of bacon when you fry him up?"

Terry has not lived enough of a life to have anything much to say, or even the tools to say it with. At twenty years of age, he was just a punk kid who recognized no authority. He is typical of enervated, ennui-ridden teenagers who have known no boundaries, taken no responsibility for their actions nor understood their consequences; they think life's answers are hidden just out of reach. He got caught before he had the chance to grow out of it.

I would say I was, pretty much, having a bad year. . . . I was doing things to impress friends and help friends. Do things to try to impress family members. Doing everything for people for all the wrong reasons. . . .

When I grew up I used to do a lot of things: take cars, break into businesses, steal cars, motorcycles, the whole nine yards. . . . I was like the center of attention. And when I'd steal something, like, a car stereo, or something, it wasn't for the money. It wasn't for the object. I'd get it and I'd end up giving it to my friends, because I thought that's what I needed to do to please them . . . to make them be my friend and make them like me.

Terry's father had had sixteen children by two wives. Terry had two children by different women.

Two of my older brothers are in the military. One's in the Marine Corps, one's in the Navy. He's a sergeant down in Key West, Florida. One of my other family members, my sister's a bus driver. My other brother works in a factory, electronic factory. My other brother is going to college, right now, for criminal law.

Maybe with so many siblings, Terry found it hard to get much attention or approval. Maybe he simply got lost in the crowd. But seeking forbidden thrills and exhibiting asocial behavior to get noticed usually backfires.

. . . being afraid how my father would feel that I got my brother involved. My younger brother was my father's—hate to say it—apple of his eye. My father's life revolved around my little brother. To have one son taken away was devastating but, to have two at once is a total big loss. And at my father's age and everything. My brother Duane was all he had left living in the house with him.

Or maybe, being the son of a cop, Terry thought he was above the law and could avoid the consequences of his sprees. Perhaps the pressures of being a juvenile in today's world contributed to his irresponsible behavior. Until the murder, Terry had been charged only with misdemeanors.

We discovered an eerie coincidence in Terry's background. We had gone to Connecticut to meet with Michael Ross as well as Terry Johnson. As it turns out, the two men are connected by more than just death row.

My father was a police officer when Michael Ross got arrested. He lived in the same town that I did. . . . They moved him out of his apartment and everything. My brother rented his apartment—same exact apartment and I went and stayed with my brother quite a bit. . . . Kind of, go test the well water, you know.

We also learned Terry had done a short stint in the National Guard. That might explain his erect posture, his machine-gun responses, and his clipped sentence structure. His long hair was a concession to his rebel tendencies.

Terry shared his philosophy about prison.

It shows that everybody can make mistakes. Everybody gets in trouble. Jail isn't prejudiced. It lets in white, Black, Indian, Hispanic, Mexican, thin, fat, strong, short, men, women, and children. Jail is not prejudiced. There's no certain quota, or certain criteria for it, other than somebody being in jail.

When somebody hears of a crime and they hear of somebody being on death row, the first thing they think of is like, Charles Manson. Somebody deranged, lunatic. They pick up the paper and they say, "Man, if I ever saw that dude on the street, I'd know for sure that he was a monster." It's not that way, at all.

And with that revelation, at such a young age, he has been shoved into adulthood. He had been headed for trouble, had embarked long ago down the wrong path. Now one event defined his entire life.

Lorie asked him what he would say if he had a chance to talk to his victim's family.

I wouldn't know where to begin. I wouldn't know where to end. But, an apology. I know an apology is never going to cut it . . . not going to cut it. But, still, you want to be able to talk to somebody and let them see the side that . . . a different side than what the media prints or what the TV, newspapers all say about you because they're just going to say the stuff that's going to sell newspapers and make people watch. The meaner you are and the more heartless you are, the more people are going to get more into it and hate you more, buy their newspapers and sit down and watch the television.

Throughout the interview, Terry said all the right things. He stood before us in the little prison courtroom, with shackles on his legs, and expressed sorrow for his actions. He was maybe a little too sincere. Had he learned how to push the right buttons since he was arrested?

Lorie steered the conversation toward the subject of death. Did he avoid thinking about it?

No, because it seems like I'm sitting on the edge of it, right now. It's like you're walking a tight-wire and you know that, sooner or later, you can fall. And it could be two years from now, five years from now, ten years from now. But, it's still on your mind that it can happen and it's inevitable that, in so many years, it's going to happen.

His answer seemed a bit too fast, too pat. Terry was not the first person we had met on death row whose emotional maturity was less developed than his chronological age would suggest. But for each of us childhood ends the moment we realize we can die.

Terry is not in immediate danger. "In Connecticut, the death penalty is basically symbolic," says Eric Freedman, who teaches constitutional law and legal history at Hofstra University. "No one has been executed, and no one is near execution."

DANIEL WEBB

Nᴼ 124596

Somers Correctional Institution
Somers, Connecticut

Year of birth	1961
Marital status	single
Children	none
Date of offense	August 24, 1989
Sentenced to death	July 26, 1991
Status	under appeal

Daniel Webb was sentenced to death for the murder of bank vice president Diane Gellenbeck, whom he kidnapped from a Hartford parking garage in 1989. Webb took her to a nearby park and raped her, then shot her five times when she attempted to escape. At trial Webb was generally uncooperative with defense attorneys. He refused to express remorse for his crimes, and did not attend court on the day the jury's verdict was announced.

Source: *Hartford Courant*, 2 December 1995, 26 July 1991.

Early one morning in 1988 I was occupying a postage-stamp-size room in Kyoto, Japan. It must have been around 2:00 A.M. when I started to spin the television dial. I stopped at a BBC documentary, only half in English, on the death penalty. Despite an early morning appointment only a few hours away, I was mesmerized by the film; I could not take my eyes off the small TV screen. Although the film was in color, the subject matter was black and white.

Months later I learned that the film was called *Fourteen Days in May*. It was about the last two weeks in the life of Edward Earl Johnson, who was put to death in Mississippi's gas chamber in 1987. I tracked it down and now own a copy. The cinéma vérité opus served as the catalyst for my project.

Driving up to the Connecticut Correctional Institute at Somers reminded me of the opening scene of *Fourteen Days in May*. Only the Japanese subtitles were missing. Mile after mile of green, rolling hills passed by. Fence posts blurred hypnotically in the car window. Then the sprawling prison complex rose out of the soft landscape.

Somers is an affluent town nestled in idyllic rural surroundings; it is rumored that because the prison population is included in its census figures, the town is awarded federal funding as if it were economically disadvantaged. The citizens don't like the prison in their midst but they don't complain about whatever government money comes their way.

I had made the trip the preceding week when we photographed Michael Ross, so I had had an opportunity to scout the location. For this visit I had requested permission to use the large visiting room, and the administration had granted it. It would make a stunning tableau. We could have the room to ourselves for only a limited time, though. Families had traveled a long way to see their loved ones. I knew the guards would be constantly checking their watches; I'd be in a race against the clock.

The room proved perfect; it was a scene straight out of an old Alfred Hitchcock film. On visiting days, when the room was full, it was a microcosm of the American Dream gone wrong. Now, for me, it would be empty. We quickly set up our equipment.

We awaited patiently for Daniel Webb's entrance. Tall and muscular, he stood almost six feet, three inches tall and weighed about 190 pounds. A rottweiler of a man—thick, deliberate, large-jawed, massive shouldered—he was the most physically imposing of all the men I photographed. Webb sat in the stadium-sized room like a boxer, with his corner men—the guards and the prison psychologist—scrutinizing his every move.

We had to abort the interview sooner than I would have liked. Though we spent a couple of hours in that room, I felt we had whisked Webb in and out. The audiotape we made didn't reveal much

about him, either. The photographs superseded the conversation and I regret it.

Ever since I had seen *Fourteen Days in May*, I had dreamed of shooting on death row. Now, six years later, I was there. Though my vision had been clear from the beginning, I still struggled with what I saw around me. The more I heard prisoners speak of their lives and crimes, the less I was able to tell truth from fiction. The ambiguity has increased with each roll of film exposed.

Though Webb had done time for a similar crime, he maintains his innocence of the murder of Diane Gellenbeck. He claims he was forced by an incompetent defense attorney and an inept judge to defend himself in the court. I find it inconceivable that a judge would tolerate a defendant representing himself in a life-or-death situation. But I know that innocence, ineffective counsel, and politically motivated judges are common in death-penalty cases. I wonder, just a little, if any of those elements is found in this case.

Every death-row inmate changes to some degree during his time there, so that the man who is killed is not the one who committed the crime. *Fourteen Days in May* showed the courage that Edward Earl Johnson was somehow able to muster during his final hours. Nevertheless, the walk to the death chamber is not a heroic voyage; we must not be seduced into thinking it is.

DUNCAN PEDER McKENZIE, JR.

Nº A013790

Montana State Prison   Deer Lodge, Montana

Year of birth	1953
Marital status	widowed
Children	three
Date of offense	January 21, 1974
Sentenced to death	March 3, 1975
Status	executed May 10, 1995, by lethal injection

The murder of twenty-three-year-old Lana Harding, a teacher in a rural area near Conrad, Montana, was the crime that brought Duncan McKenzie, Jr., to death row. McKenzie had kidnapped Harding from her home at the Pioneer School, raped and then strangled her near to death, and finally beaten her until she died. McKenzie had served a previous prison sentence for assault and had only recently moved into the area. He was arrested after police learned that his truck had been seen at the school on the evening of the crime.

McKenzie spent over twenty years appealing his sentence before he was executed in 1995. Among those to witness his death was Harding's mother, Ethel, who had by then been elected to the state senate.

Source: *State v McKenzie*, 557 P2d 1,023 (1977); *New York Times*, 11 May 1995, 23 July 1990; *Dallas Morning News*, 9 May 1995.

In his twenty years on death row, Duncan McKenzie gave almost no interviews. When it appeared certain he was going to die, requests for an audience poured in. He granted just two.

. . . actually, you folks and the guy from the *Dallas Morning News* are the only people who have approached who did not have some kind of hidden agenda that they wanted to exploit or whatever. I guess it's nice to know that there's other people out there besides what I've had to deal with for the local news.

The execution was such big news, the local newspapers treated us like minor celebrities. Somehow everyone seemed to know we were coming to town. We were nervous and I had no idea what kind of reception to expect. Under cover of darkness, we skulked into town at 2:00 A.M. The state of Montana had given us last-minute approval to interview McKenzie while the prison was in pre-execution lockdown. The timing was inconvenient for us—we needed seven days to get cheaper airfares. How absurd: pinching pennies when someone is scheduled to die.

The weather that week turned ugly. We drove from Helena through pea-soup fog and horizontal snow.

Every death-row encounter makes you jaded, especially when you deal with prison hierarchy. Handshakes and nods are no longer casual. We were put through the compulsory ceremony of logging our equipment through security, then we were taken out to the prison courtyard. As we carried our photographic and recording equipment across the yard, we unexpectedly bumped into McKenzie, who was being escorted to maximum security. After all the negotiations over whether we could be in the same room with him, there we were, side by side in the open air. No one even acknowledged anyone else. Though I knew it was almost certainly against the rules, I grabbed Duncan's right hand, which was cuffed to his waist. In obvious pain from a slipped disk, he limped as I walked by his side to the entrance of the building. When we reached the inner sanctum, they separated us.

We were reunited in the guards' cafeteria, which had been set up as a makeshift interview room. At the time we met, McKenzie had beaten the devil, maneuvering through eight execution dates and myriad postconviction appeals. He had lived the last twenty years in defiance of state-sanctioned death—the second-longest time under the death sentence of anyone in the United States.

Well, I'll either be executed Wednesday morning sometime or I will have my sentence commuted to life without parole which, being alive, has a lot of benefits to it but being alive in a place like this has a lot of drawbacks to it so . . .

I've got kids out there that I haven't seen in years and some that don't want to see me. . . . You're existing from one day to the next, waiting for the court process to go through. . . . It's so monotonous. . . . You've done this for almost twenty-one years and even though the system, which is imperfect, is there, it's a system that completely failed in Montana.

One of my assistants, Courtney Bent, nervously tried to coax a bit of background out of McKenzie. He told us that in his youth, he had driven his father to rodeos long before he earned a driver's license. He had nursed his father's frequent hangovers. In exchange, his father had taught him to be an auto mechanic.

I could fly a plane. I could fly a helicopter. I could repair just about any vehicle, rebuild it and put it back together. I couldn't do that now. There's too much computer-coordinated equipment out there.

Then McKenzie broached the subject of death.

Someone who I had a great deal of trust in at the time, and who's died since, told me that death should not be feared. That each night when we go to sleep we dream for a certain period of time. Sometimes our subconscious and our conscience will remember the dream or a portion of it. When we're not dreaming, there's a void. It's just emptiness. We don't know it's there. It's just part of the nights as it goes by. It's a little slice of death and yet . . . we don't fear going to sleep. . . .

We fear only what we don't know or fear itself.

Courtney kept probing, and Duncan went on.

The way I look at it—death—it's something we have to accept whether we want to or not because from the day we're born to the day of our death, we're dying. All of us. . . .

He went on as if time meant nothing. He talked at his feet. No excess motion, no flamboyant gestures, except to wince at the pain in his back. He had rehearsed the things he said, at least in his mind; I had read some of the same comments in the newspapers. His words were dispassionate. Maybe as someone in his last hours his mind was

on automatic pilot. Maybe he was tired and had given up. It was the fifth of May, and he had five days left to live.

Finally he touched on his victim, Lana Harding.

I've heard nothing but wonderful things about Lana Harding as long as I've been here. So, I can't say anything bad about her or her mother for that matter. I can understand her grief and her anger because she sustained a terrible loss. My wife and I went through a similar loss. Our first daughter died a crib death at six months and what made it even more bizarre was that the day that she died, we had taken her for her six-month checkup and the doctor . . . if all the kids were as healthy as she was, he'd be out of business.

As we listened to McKenzie, the guards made derisive remarks about his veracity. This had been a fairly common occurrence during our sessions at various institutions. They didn't understand our purpose, but they knew they made us uncomfortable, and they enjoyed that.

The next day we were invited to the clemency hearing. Deer Lodge is a small town where the modern and the old-fashioned clash. TV cameras and anchor persons faced an audience of weathered faces topped by baseball caps and cowboy hats. A mounted moose head hung on the back wall, and children ran loose. On the left side of the courtroom sat those who were against the death penalty; on the right, friends of the victim's mother. Everybody knew each other on both sides of the aisle. The police guards hugged the walls.

Walking through the prison that evening, I caught sight of McKenzie talking through a partition to his family and his lawyers. They were bringing him the news that the hearing had gone badly. I waved through the glass. Four days to go.

Lethal injection is now the method of execution in Montana. The state's death chamber is actually an RV. Witnesses to the execution sit at the feet of the condemned. The executioner allowed McKenzie to listen to country music on a Walkman as he received the lethal injection. It was a Marty Robbins tape.

For a brief period Duncan was the most famous man in the state—front page. He was the first man to be executed since FDR was in office. By the time I got my film developed, he had been buried.

LESTER KILLS ON TOP

N⁰ A027079

Montana State Prison   Deer Lodge, Montana

Year of birth	1962
Marital status	single
Children	unknown
Date of offense	October 17, 1987
Sentenced to death	June 24, 1988
Status	pending resentencing

Shortly after midnight on October 17, 1987, two brothers, Lester and Vern Kills On Top, entered a bar in Miles City Montana. With them were two women, Diane Bull Coming and Doretta Four Bear. When another patron, John Martin Etchemendy, complained he could not find his car, the four offered to help. With Etchemendy in their car, they drove away from the bar.

At some point the four decided to assault and rob the victim. They forced Etchemendy to disrobe and climb into the trunk of the car. At 5:00 A.M. Four Bear left the group, but another friend, Lavonne Quiroz, joined it. The group drove south to Gillette, Wyoming, arriving there in the afternoon. While Vern and Quiroz went to a bar, Lester and Bull Coming drove out of town. They stopped, and according to Diane's testimony, Lester beat Etchemendy to death with a pipe. They abandoned the body in a rural area twenty miles south of Gillette.

Source: *Lester Kills On Top v State*, 901 P2d 1,368 (1995); *State v Lester Kills On Top*, 787 P2d 336 (1990); *State v Vern Kills On Top*, 793 P2d 1,273 (1990).

Once the Blackfoot, Crow, Sioux, and Assiniboine roamed Montana's plains. When white settlers invaded the area in the nineteenth century, the Cheyenne became embroiled in wars to defend their territory. By the late twentieth century, only about two thousand northern Cheyenne were left. They live on the Tongue River reservation, located in the southeastern part of Montana. This story is about two of them, Lester and Vern Kills On Top, full-blooded, enrolled members of the northern Cheyenne tribe.

The guards told us Lester had cut his long hair for the camera. He wore a bright fluorescent-orange jumpsuit and prison-issue disposable slippers. Small and slight, he was not what I had expected.

Access to Lester was closely guarded by a lawyer in Washington state. A long list of restrictions had been faxed to us, including a prohibition against recording our conversation with him. We set about convincing the officer in charge to remove Lester's handcuffs. But once they were off, Lester became uncomfortable. He had not sat with civilians in a long time; freedom made him nervous. When we went out into the hallway, his handcuffs went back on.

Lester's disposition was delicate, so his attorneys had asked us not to talk about his crime. We skirted around it, taking care not to upset or depress him. Lester cannot read or watch TV: his attention wanders. We were told he paces constantly inside his minuscule cell, a caged soul.

Although Lester now fervently embraces Christianity, studying the Bible in prison, he was educated in Native American lore. Named Strange Owl by his grandfather, he speaks and reads Cheyenne. But like many Indians today, Lester had had alcoholic parents, and had been shuttled back and forth among several foster families, both on and off the reservation. But Indian mores often clash with western culture and he was not always accepted by his people.

On a map, Miles City, where their crime began, is about two finger-widths away from the reservation. Because the Kills On Top brothers committed part of their crime off the reservation and part on Indian territory, the murder of John Martin Etchemendy became a question of jurisdiction. With Etchemendy in the trunk of their car, the men drove around southern Montana and northern Wyoming, cut through the reservation, and crossed the border. There was therefore a great deal of legal maneuvering over where they should be tried: in Wyoming or Montana, in federal court or state court. Returning Lester to Indian jurisdiction was not seriously considered. Because Lester had murdered a member of the white majority on majority land, the majority took over and punished him according to majority law.

In mid-1995, the *Montana Independent Record* carried the headline "Convict's Death Sentence Overturned." The state supreme court had ordered a resentencing for Lester Kills On Top. I had always been bewildered that although the state's key witness had been involved in the crime, she had never been prosecuted. Now Lester's lawyer had convinced the Montana Supreme Court that the state had withheld evidence that might have undermined her credibility. Lester was off death row—at least for a while.

Vern Kills On Top

Nº A27177

Montana State Prison   Deer Lodge, Montana

Year of birth	1961
Marital status	single
Children	none
Date of offense	October 17, 1987
Sentenced to death	June 24, 1988
Status	under appeal

Vern Kills On Top was convicted with his brother Lester of the murder of John Martin Etchemendy, whom they met at a bar in Miles City, Montana. On the pretense of helping Etchemendy to find his car, the two men had offered him a ride. Later, forcing him into the trunk of their car, they drove him south to Gillette, Wyoming. There Vern went to a bar, while Lester and a friend drove out of town with Etchemendy still in the trunk. The body was found in a rural area twenty miles south of Gillette.

Source: *Lester Kills On Top v State*, 901 P2d 1,368 (1995); *State v Vern Kills On Top*, 793 P2d 1,273 (1990); *State v Lester Kills On Top*, 787 P2d 336 (1990).

Montana is a land of beautiful scenery, but we were not there for the ambiance. We crossed railroad tracks, passed a decrepit grain silo and abandoned trucks. The flat, open badlands stretched on that rainsoaked day to the prison's front gates.

No matter what time of day we entered these prisons, it was always night inside. Vern Kills On Top stepped out of the shadows at the end of his cellblock and shuffled forward, arms and legs hobbled by chains. As he came closer I could make out the Indian features: round face, broad nose, raven-colored hair.

Native American culture clashes with contemporary society; outsiders are invariably suspect. From the moment he entered the cramped, makeshift canteen to the end of our visit hours later, Vern Kills On Top had little to say. I am rarely at ease when I meet residents of death row, and Vern made no effort to make it easier. His attitude became an obstruction. His eyes darted around the dirty little room, following intently every move we made. When my assistant, Ken MacEwen, walked behind him, Vern's head swiveled like an owl's. Everything distracted him. With each interruption, he escaped us.

I tried to coax Vern by relating childhood experiences—summers on the farm riding horses, adolescent memories. He matched me experience for experience, but never relaxed and opened up. I never did figure out whether it was his indigenous side or his prison facade that was frustrating me. Vern Kills On Top does not consider himself a citizen; he considers himself a Cheyenne.

I persevered. Slowly, something began to change. Though the only voice I heard was Courtney Bent's, each hush became a kind of speech. Vern's limited discourse was like modern jazz, sparse and abstract. By his silence, he told me about the chasm between us. The silence *was* his message.

Slowly I began to understand, or at least make some sense of it. Prison had reduced Vern's voice to a single note—suspicion. Native Americans have always been wary of photographs; maybe their suspicions are well founded. I respected the cultural distance. We had to piece together whatever fragments he involuntarily revealed.

Courtney was so taken with Cheyenne lore that she asked the authorities if they could bring Vern back, so we could record his dialect. Vern was as surprised as we were when permission was granted. Self-consciously, he spoke the beautiful Cheyenne words into our microphone.

We walked out of Vern's windowless night. He was our last inmate; the project was "done." I knew I would never come back.